Chinese Leadership

Chinese Leadership

Barbara Xiaoyu Wang
Programme Director and China Representative at Ashridge Business School, UK

and

Harold Chee
Programme Director at Ashridge Business School, UK

First published 2011 by
PALGRAVE MACMILLAN

Palgrave Macmillan in the UK is an imprint of Macmillan Publishers Limited, registered in England, company number 785998, of Houndmills, Basingstoke, Hampshire RG21 6XS.

Palgrave Macmillan in the US is a division of St Martin's Press LLC, 175 Fifth Avenue, New York, NY 10010.

Palgrave Macmillan is the global academic imprint of the above companies and has companies and representatives throughout the world.

Palgrave® and Macmillan® are registered trademarks in the United States, the United Kingdom, Europe and other countries.

ISBN 978–0–230–24818–2

This book is printed on paper suitable for recycling and made from fully managed and sustained forest sources. Logging, pulping and manufacturing processes are expected to conform to the environmental regulations of the country of origin.

A catalogue record for this book is available from the British Library.

A catalog record for this book is available from the Library of Congress.

10   9   8   7   6   5   4   3   2   1
20   19   18   17   16   15   14   13   12   11

Printed and bound in Great Britain by
CPI Antony Rowe, Chippenham and Eastbourne

Contents

Figures and Tables

Foreword

The challenges of leadership get even bigger when the members of the team you're leading come from different backgrounds and different cultures to your own. For the new expatriate manager in China there is much to learn. Whilst in many of the China's cities, the architecture and infrastructure give the misleading impression that one could be almost anywhere in the world, there are, very close to the surface, layers of "Chinese-ness" which can often be difficult to comprehend.

Today there are more and more overseas companies coming to China to invest, trade or to provide services. As China becomes stronger, there is less willingness on the part of Chinese business partners and staff to merely accept the norms and behaviors of the overseas company and therefore it becomes increasingly important that the expatriate manager understands and can empathize with his Chinese counterparts.

Furthermore, many Chinese companies are offering real competition for many products and services. In order to counter this, the foreign company has to be able to operate effectively in this changing market. They need to have a better understanding of the Chinese than they did 15–20 years ago.

I have the pleasure of knowing Barbara and Harold for a long time. Not only do they have first-hand experience of working in China; but also tremendous experience in teaching "Western" management concepts and practice to groups of Chinese managers and sharing their insights into Chinese business culture with Western managers. In the first part of this book, they have eloquently captured the fundamentals of Chinese business culture and its philosophical roots. In the second part of the book, they build on this cultural base and provide sound advice on the actual practice of managing in China

I have worked in international, multicultural environments nearly all my working life and have spent the last ten years working with the China–Britain Business Council in Beijing. We provide advice and assistance to British companies entering or working in the China market. I strongly recommend this book to the many new managers and leaders who will come to China or work with Chinese companies outside China.

Brian Outlaw,
Executive Director,
China Britain Business Council,
Beijing, China. 2011.

Introduction

China, as we all know, is booming. This book is an attempt to look at one aspect of that boom, leadership. Are there styles of leadership particular to China? If so, what are they? How do they work? And are they transferable to international organizations? For international business seeking to build a presence in China, what kind of leadership will their Chinese employees expect? What kind of leadership will work best?

At a deeper level still, there is a debate about how China itself can lead the world, not just economically but morally. The old Western model is looking ever more dented since Enron, Worldcom and the greed-driven crisis of 2008. In response to this opportunity, China has begun to re-examine its mighty intellectual traditions, especially Confucianism and Buddhism.

In truth, these traditional cultural values have always shaped leadership and management practices in China and in countries influenced by it. For example, when Redding (1982) and Franke, Hofstede and Bond (1991) looked at what were then termed the "Asian Tiger" economies of Singapore, Taiwan, South Korea and Hong Kong, they established a close link between economic development and Confucianism.

The Confucian focus on the "soft" side of society is aptly summed up in an old Chinese proverb:

> If you want one year of prosperity, cultivate grains.
> If you want ten years of prosperity, cultivate trees.
> If you want one hundred years of prosperity, cultivate
> PEOPLE.

The focus of this book is twofold. Firstly, our attention will be on how Chinese leadership is very much influenced by traditional Chinese philosophies and value systems – not just those of Confucius – and on the impact this has on the workplace. Secondly, we will look at Western concepts of management and leadership, and see how they need to be adapted to work in the Chinese context: Western leaders in China may find that what made them successful and effective back home may not work in their new setting. This is a practical book to help leaders and managers working in China learn how to manage a workforce that has a different cultural mindset, and to show them how to do so sensitively and empathetically.

The book is divided into two parts. Part 1 consists of five chapters with a focus on the background of Chinese philosophy and the cultural environment. Chapter 1 explores the philosophical roots of Chinese culture; Chapter 2 looks at these philosophical movements and their impact on leadership styles; Chapter 3 covers some of the key core cultural features that impact not just leadership behavior but also everyday life in Chinese society; Chapter 4 explores some of the leadership challenges of working in such a culturally diverse environment; finally, Chapter 5 describes different types of commercial organization in China, and the different leadership styles and challenges relevant to them.

The main focus of Part 2 is on how to make it happen. Its five chapters explore some of the major Western leadership and management concepts in detail, ways in which these concepts are perceived by the Chinese and the ways they can best be adapted and utilized in China. Chapters 6 to 10 cover communications, team management, delegation and decision-making, negotiations and coaching.

There has to be a health warning on any literature dealing with China and the Chinese: China has been a land of myth, mystery and exaggeration for the West since Marco Polo came back to thirteenth-century Venice with tales of cities of a million people (unheard of in those days), unimaginable wealth, exotic food and strange customs. Maybe the only consistent theme in the West's perception of China has been its inconsistency, or rather a Western desire to see in China what it wants to see. As traveler Stephen King-Hall said in 1924:

> "China" and "the Chinese" are words which embrace so vast a subject that any attempt to set out details inevitably obscures the main features of the subject.... China, like statistics, can be made to supply apparent proof for any preconceived notion.

Back in 1924, that did not matter over-much, except to the relatively few people involved in the China trade. But now the problem is serious: now we have to understand the real differences between China and the West, to bring about the mutual benefits, the "win–win outcomes," that both cultures desire. This book is designed to make these more likely.

We would like to express our gratitude to Chris West for his editorial support and contribution; to Zhang Jianning, Campbell Thompson and Peng Ningke, who reviewed the manuscript, kindly corrected our errors and provided insightful comments. We regret that we are unable to acknowledge individually every person who has assisted us, but we would like to express our gratitude to all those who have helped us, for their contribution, patience and support during the time it took us to write this book. A special note of thanks to Eleanor Davey Corrigan and her editorial team for their support and encouragement. Last but not least, we would like to extend our appreciation and warmest thanks to Stephen Rutt at Palgrave Macmillan, who commissioned this book and had the patience to see the project through.

Barbara Xiaoyu Wang
Harold Chee
Ashridge Business School, 2011

Part I
Foundations of Chinese Leadership

1
Chinese Culture: A Brief History

One cannot understand Chinese concepts of leadership without understanding Chinese culture. And to understand the culture, it is necessary to go back 7,000 years. This may come as something of a shock to anyone who regards the era before the Internet as prehistory, but it is true. So, let's begin the journey...

YI JING, THE BOOK OF CHANGES

Yi Jing, or the Book of Changes, is recognized as the origin of Chinese philosophy, culture and science. Legend has it that three sages contributed to this book over a period of 4,500 years. The first was Fu Xi, a mythical figure (he had a human head and a serpent's body) who created eight hexagrams 7,000 years ago. The aim was to predict natural phenomena by using eight symbols (combinations of three lines) to represent eight core astronomical and geographical conditions. Zhou Wenwang (1152–1056 BC), a genuine historical figure, developed the model to 64 hexagrams and added commentary. Finally, Confucius (551–479 BC) – of whom we will hear much more – added further commentary.

The superficial purpose of the hexagrams is divination. But at a deeper level, the *Yi Jing* is many things: it is a philosophical book that teaches a method of dialectic thinking in a constantly changing macro- and micro-environment; it is a scientific book, outlining principles of astronomy, meteorology and physics; and it is a social treatise on how to interact with others and behave

Figure 1.1 *The eight hexagrams*

correctly in different situations. However, it delivers its messages in a coded way, and can only be understood by people who care to work out the code and the messages.

Throughout the millennia of Chinese civilization, *Yi Jing* has been used and misused in many ways. If philosophers and rulers have lived by it, so have crooks and fortune-tellers. In the modern world, the book is being rediscovered with exactly the same range of results. Philosophers used it to help understand life; *feng shui* "consultants" use it to add plausibility to their practices.

A good summary of the key concepts of the *Yi Jing* comes from Nan Huaijin, a great Sinologue who has witnessed the evolution of China over the past nine decades with deep understanding. At the heart of the model, he sees three principles:

- *Change*: Everything in the cosmos is changing constantly: space, time, human beings (physically and mentally), and so on.

- *Simplicity*: There is a rule underlining all these changes which would make it possible for people to understand all phenomena – however we have either lost or never possessed the wisdom to capture it.

- *Eternity*: There is a "thing" which is the core of the Cosmos. Unchanging itself, it drives all changes. In the West, it is seen as "God"; in Chinese philosophy, it is "*dào*." (It is also the "ultimate truth" of ancient Greek philosophy.)

In addition to these three principles, there are three methodologies, three ways of asking questions:

- *Reason*: There is a reason for everything: life, emotions, thinking, behavior, physical movement, astronomical changes…Applying this approach, for instance, to a tape recorder, we would ask what it was for.

- *Form*: the physical outlook and visible appearance. Applying this approach to a tape recorder, we would describe its shape, color and so on.

- *Quantitative relations*: measurement in numbers. Applying this to the recorder, we would look at specifications such as power usage or the number of minutes the tape can last.

Clearly, in this brief introduction we cannot go into this fascinating text in proper detail. It is sufficient for now to point out certain basic ideas in it. Change is perpetual and all-pervasive. But it is not random: behind all changes lie clear, objective principles – but ones that we do not fully understand. Wisdom lies in adapting one's actions to the underlying state of the universe as revealed by the hexagrams: given the perpetual and mysterious change in things, superficial consistency is not a virtue. Another key aspect of the *Yi Jing* is that it is ultimately not a theoretical treatise but a practical tool, designed for use, for solving problems in the world.

THE FIVE GREAT SCHOOLS

Among the hundreds of schools of thought in Chinese history, we will explore five major ones. These are, in sequence of their emergence, Confucianism, Mohism, Daoism, Legalism and Militarism. These form the "DNA" of Chinese culture and leadership, even today, 25 centuries after their initial emergence. They are complementary in some ways but contradictory in others, and Chinese people tend to apply different philosophies in different circumstances (as the *Yi Jing* recommends). This explains the diversity of the Chinese leadership style, which often confuses Westerners. In the first two chapters we will try to put the reader under the Chinese skin so they can feel and experience this hereditary force.

It is not too much to say that Confucius was the torchbearer of Chinese civilization. He was the first great Chinese philosopher to make his teachings available and relevant to all classes of society, from aristocrats to slaves. The other great originator is Lao Zi, the founder of Daoism. Of the five philosophies we shall look at, four are essentially based on, or arguments against, Confucianism. For this reason, they share common beliefs:

- "*Dào*" (the Way) is the ultimate truth to pursue.

- The dynamic of *Yīn–Yáng*, Heaven, earth and the human is critical for all processes. In Western terms, it means that the right time, the right place and the right people are the key factors in success.

- The view of humaneness, holism and dialecticism.

All the schools seek to provide models for leadership from their different perspectives.

Confucianism

Confucianism focuses on personal benevolence and an ethical, harmonious, but very stratified society. Apart from Confucius, Meng Zi (372–289 BC) and Xun Zi (313–238 BC) also contributed to this school.

Confucius was the illegitimate child of an impoverished aristocrat, born during a period of strife between Chinese states. As an adult, he travelled among these states, trying to mediate and make peace. He was not hugely successful at this: he lived in relative poverty and drifted from place to place preaching his ideas.

The aim of the Confucian is to establish a harmonious, rational and hierarchical society, where everyone follows the rules in accordance with their political and social status. The philosophy of Confucius was that to achieve this, the country should be governed not by law but by ethics. What mattered most was individual self-cultivation. The ruler – who possessed his role by divine right – should practice this, too, and command the people with morality and humanity.

Education lay at the heart of Confucius's philosophy: teachers in China still enjoy status and respect because Confucius glorified their occupation.

Confucius was also very prolific, editing many pre-existing books on politics, religion, mythology, literature, music, social etiquette, philosophy and history. He compiled textbooks which were used as compulsory education in China for thousands of years, until the early twentieth century. His own thought is gathered in a work called the *Analects*, a relatively short book of fewer than 11,000 characters (though his admirers say that "half of the *Analects* is good enough to govern the world").

Confucianism slowly became the dominant ideology in China, being canonized four hundred years after his death, in the Han Dynasty (around 140 BC). From it comes the theory of "Humane Leadership" which is favored by professional officials and leaders at State Owned Enterprises (SOEs), and which we will discuss further in Chapter 2.

Despite the power of Confucianism, it is a mistake to assume that it is the only philosophy that matters in Chinese leadership. (Western analysts, used to monotheistic cultures, often make this mistake.) Let us move on to look at other essential influences.

Mohism

Mohism is the philosophy of Mo Zi (468–376 BC). Unlike the other philosophers listed here, Mo Zi came from a slave family. His "grassroots-driven" philosophy focuses on universal love and nonviolence, and aims for world peace. Unlike Confucian love, which is to be applied strictly in the context of hierarchy, Mo Zi's love is for everyone. "One's love is to others' parents what one's love is to one's own parents" is a famous quote of his, which led to him being called an animal by other philosophers for not loving his own parents most. Confucius's injunction to "love parents" is understood to mean that one should love one's own parents, that they are superior to others' parents; that the degree of love is different. But Mo Zi's injunction to "love parents" means one should love others' parents equally as one loves one's own; therefore there is no difference in the two types of love for Mo Zi.

In the modern world Mohism was espoused by revolutionaries and communists. Mo Zi was a hero for the ordinary man or woman, and his ideas were also applied in secret societies. Not surprisingly, Mohism was despised by other traditional schools.

Mohism provides the rationale for Altruistic Theory, which tends to favor junior employees.

Daoism

Daoism is the most mystical of the great Chinese philosophies. The wise person is advised to contemplate nature, and especially water, which appears soft and colorless but which actually sustains all life and wears away mountains over time. For the Daoist, "the weak prevail over the strong, and the supple overcome all restraint." It is the lofty ideal of the reclusive liberal, romantic and pessimistic about the value of action.

The founder of Daoism, Lao Zi, lived around 570 BC. He was an official, but later retired to become a hermit, wrote one book, the *Dao De Jing*, then disappeared – according to legend, because he became immortal. Lao Zi said, "I have three treasures, the first is compassion, the second is frugality and the third is not daring to take the lead in anything." His philosophy is about divining the "ultimate truth" called *dào*, the natural law of both the cosmos and the human world, and adapting oneself to it.

Daoism is against hierarchical society. Its core philosophy of leadership is "laissez-faire": the leader should step back and let his or her followers achieve things in their own way. Lao Zi said, "The way to govern a country is like cooking a little fish, which should be slow and tender without drastic changes."

Daoism's main concepts form the basis of the Naturalistic Theory outlined in Chapter 2.

Legalism

Legalism focuses on rigorous law and regulation as well as fair reward and punishment.

Li Kui (455–395 BC) wrote the *Book of Law*, which provides the foundation of Legalism. Shang Yang (390–338 BC) and Han Fei (280–233 BC) finally consummated this important school of philosophy, which is not only the foundation of the Chinese feudal political system but also a key philosophy for current Chinese leaders.

Unlike Confucians, Legalists believe in the essential badness of human nature. To govern a country efficiently, they propose a strict legal system and severe punishment. This should be implemented without exception: "The prince is to be punished as same as to the plebeian for violating the law," said Shang Yang. By contrast, Confucianism granted privilege to the ruling class. Ironically, both Shang Yang and Han Fei were eventually executed by their rulers.

Legalism was a very effective doctrine in times of chaos and turbulence. Qin Shihuang, the First Emperor of China, terminated half a century of civil war and unified the country by adhering to the Legalist philosophy. And over 2,000 years later, Mao effectively did the same thing. However, both Emperor Qin and Mao failed to consolidate their triumph; the former's dynasty died with him, and the latter failed to implant his ideology into Chinese life.

Confucianism is about long-term stabilization and sustainability; Legalism is short-term and about sovereignty. Confucian leaders prefer to educate and inspire people to gain their commitment, creating followers by setting a moral and personal example; Legalists force people into compliance.

The key concepts of Legalism form the basis of Institutional Theory, outlined in Chapter 2.

Militarism

Militarism provides a balance between moral-driven Confucianism and law-driven Legalism, by focusing on pragmatic stratagems.

There are several founders of this school, but Sun Zi is the best known, thanks to his book *The Art of War*. This is one of the three books called the "Tripod of Chinese Culture," along with Confucius's *Analects* and Lao Zi's *Dao De Jing*. Not surprisingly, *The Art of War* is more popular than the other two in the West due to its immediate practical applicability. Novelist James Clavell believed that if Western leaders had read it, World Wars I and II would have been avoided. It is also a favorite of bestselling marketing author Philip Kotler.

Historically, since the Qin Dynasty (220 BC), the philosophy of Militarism has not been valued much in China. This is for several reasons. Firstly in a unified, peaceful China, Confucianism, Legalism and Daoism had more relevance. Secondly, Militarism was (unfairly) perceived as superficial, as a series of tricks for resorting to expediency and playing politics. Thirdly, the ruling class was afraid that common people would take advantage of it to overthrow them. Indeed, Mao Zedong used it to win a 20-year guerrilla war.

In this book, we will focus only on the leadership perspective of Militarism, which is Strategic Theory, described in the next chapter.

Confucianism vs. Daoism

Confucius was about twenty years junior to Lao Zi. They met once: Confucius went to consult Lao Zi, but there is no record of what they discussed. It is, however, recorded that Confucius was very quiet after the meeting; he did not speak for three days, then said that, at the spiritual level, if Lao Zi was a dragon, he was just a worm.

Confucianism and Daoism share some common principles, such as benevolence, "servant heart" leadership, harmony, modesty, stability, industriousness and frugality, though they view them from different perspectives. Confucianism is a school of rationalism and pragmatism, it is people-oriented and focuses on human dynamics. Confucius never commented on the supernatural or mysterious, once observing, "I have not yet understood the mortal life, why should I understand the immortal?" In Confucianism, people should try their best to achieve what they want in a proper way: what actually happens is a matter of destiny, which is beyond rational contemplation. Confucianism is a worldly philosophy.

Daoism is romantic, naturalistic and metaphysical. It is nature-oriented and focuses on the natural dynamics of five vast forces: nature, *dào*, heaven, earth and humanity. Daoism is passive: we cannot do much, only let nature take its course. Daoism is a transcendent philosophy.

Confucianism advocates rationalism and self-cultivation, whereas Daoism prefers nature and intuition.

It is not difficult to understand why leaders prefer to use Confucianism to manage their subordinates, but prefer Daoism in their personal life. For thousands of years in China, Confucianism has been the philosophy of working and Daoism the philosophy of living. You will find two major types of decor in traditional Chinese homes. One is "happy family" paintings of women and children on porcelain and in drawings, which reflect the philosophy of Confucianism. Another is "leisure life," showing fishermen, woodsmen or eremitic intellectuals, reflecting the philosophy of Daoism.

THE EVOLUTION OF CURRENT CHINESE CULTURE

In addition to the philosophies above, Chinese culture has been deeply influenced by incoming religions, and, recently, by the culture of the West. It is important to understand that none of these imports have supplanted the old philosophies: they have just been stirred into the mixture and been allowed to brew.

Religious Influence

One of common pitfalls in understanding Chinese culture is to confuse the philosophy of Daoism and the religion of Daoism. The religion of Daoism, created by Zhang Daoling around the first century AD, is sometimes seen by outsiders as "the Chinese religion." But it never came to dominate China. Instead, other religions have had influence. Buddhism was introduced from India, also around the first century AD. Subsequent imports include Islam from Mongolia, Lamaism from Tibet, and, later, Christianity from the West. Pragmatism being a core part of Chinese culture, most Chinese adhere to a religion mainly for their personal benefit.

So, unlike many other traditions, there are no absolute, certain rules in China to guide the spiritual life. Chinese only believe what they can prove, and this impacts on the moral system – people do bad things without fear of punishment from "God" and take advantage of luck (as every individual believes he or she deserves to be the lucky one).

Western Influence to 1949

When China lost the Opium Wars (1839–1842 and 1856–1860), and the eight-power Allied Forces invaded Beijing and burned the old Summer Palace in 1900, Chinese intellectuals were shocked and confused. Why had the "Heavenly Dynasty" been defeated so easily by the "Barbarian Westerner"? They were impressed by the scientific advancement, economic development and industrial civilization of the West, and concluded that China was still sleeping on its past glory, its mindset still shackled by the old schools of philosophy. For the first time in its history Chinese intellectuals acknowledged that China needed to learn from two gentlemen from the West: Mr. D and Mr. S (alias Democracy and Science).

Following the end of the Imperial Era in 1911, the New Culture Movement was launched to stimulate new thinking to help China get out of the morass and establish a modern social and political system. Initiated by Cai Yuanpei, president of Beijing University, and Hu Shi, the guru of Chinese literature and philosophy, it set out to adopt Western culture: philosophy, lifestyle, beliefs and values. As Confucian thinking was deeply rooted in the Chinese language, Cai and Hu also used colloquial language instead of old Chinese written language. Cai studied in Germany, and was influenced by the philosophy of Schopenhauer and Kant; Hu studied in the USA and was an advocate of John Dewey's Pragmatism. Other

Chinese intellectuals were inspired by Darwin and the *Evolution and Ethics* of T. H. Huxley.

On a more popular level, Chinese cities saw a tidal wave of Western culture: English novels, Hollywood movies, French fashion and night clubs. Chinese classic language and classic philosophy were criticized and their teaching diminished in leading schools after 1920. Church schools opened in Beijing, Shanghai and Tianjin. English was taught at many Chinese universities, as were the science subjects: mathematics, logic, and physics. For the first time in Chinese history, Chinese women were permitted to have education and encouraged to work like men, though Chinese women were still struggling to have freedom to marry whom they chose.

This period of Western influence, almost exclusively confined to the cities, came to an end as China itself collapsed into anarchy, then was rescued from this state by Mao.

Soviet Influence

In 1949, Mao established Chinese socialism by adopting Marxism, implementing a unitary ideology of "Social Realism" and forbidding all other schools of thought. Although China and Russia's brotherhood broke up in 1958, the Soviet influence remains in the Chinese social system and in Chinese thinking.

Cultural Revolutionary

Mao was a teacher from a peasant family, who had profound knowledge of Chinese traditional philosophy, literature and history; he was recognized as a political leader, a strategist, a philosopher, a poet and a calligrapher. Mao didn't think that China was ready for Western democracy, but he did believe that the majority of Chinese had suffered enormously thanks to a mindset enforced by the ruling classes for 2,000 years, and he resolved to break this. The result was his "Cultural Revolution." Both "Ox-head devil" and "Snake-body spirit" (traditional and Western schools of thought) were anathematized in an attempt to "free" people's minds by unifying their thinking. Mao particularly criticized Confucianism – he actually implemented Mohism in many ways.

He effectively recast the old hierarchical structure by lowering the social status of scholars and putting blue-collar workers at the top. All traditional Chinese books were banned in schools, and the higher education system was shut down completely.

The Rise of The New Entrepreneurs

Around 1978, Deng Xiaoping reopened China to the world, focusing on economic development by encouraging people to do business. Higher education was resumed.

There were various responses to this. Some people who did not have the chance of going to university started their own businesses, and are now the backbone of modern Chinese commerce. Others studied abroad, mainly in US and UK, and stayed over: some of them became overseas returnees who made glorious returns to their hometowns twenty years later. Others went to university, graduated and worked for national or local governments; they became officials and govern China today. Still others, the majority who missed out higher education and didn't become entrepreneurs, ended up working for Chinese SOEs.

After three decades, the first true generation of businesspeople in the new China emerged, most of them in the first of the above categories. Around the early 1990s, there were a lot of complaints from Western business people about bad experiences with these people, who were perceived as dishonest. To be fair, many of these entrepreneurs had never been educated properly, academically or culturally: we see them as ignorant rather than deliberately cheating. Interestingly, most of them sent their children to study abroad in the US and UK.

In the meantime, traditional Chinese education had been largely uprooted. There were few teachers in the universities of China with a solid background of Chinese literature, history and philosophy. Hence, Chinese education focused on Western science rather than Chinese art, and demanding disciplines such as mathematics grew in importance. Unfortunately, mathematics, rather than being valued for its real use, was adopted as a major university entrance criterion and therefore became a barrier to access to higher education, as it was now essential to qualify in this discipline regardless of the type of degree pursued. The classic Chinese books written by Confucius, Lao Zi and other philosophers remained unopened, in the dungeon.

The consequence of eight decades of cultural loss in mainland China was a great deal of confusion. In contrast to the country's fast economic growth, the value system in Chinese society started going downhill. The Chinese virtues pursued by predecessors for thousands years were derided and neglected: materialism became the major pursuit for most people.

The Resurgence of Classic Philosophies

In 2005, President Hu Jintao launched the "Harmonious Society" social movement. This represents the core philosophy of Confucius. Ironically, Chinese philosophy had been popular in the West for many years: now China itself reawoke to an awareness of its national treasury. Suddenly, there were numerous lectures, forums and seminars about traditional Chinese philosophy. Primary schools started to teach classic Chinese philosophical textbooks.

In 2007 Confucianism was officially rehabilitated, and the main campus of the Confucian School was established, for the first time in the sage's homeland, in Beijing – a long way after the 140 or more Confucian schools founded in over 50 other countries. The twenty-first century sees Confucianism surviving as a major ideology in China.

Confucianism has even entered the statute books. For Confucius, filial piety was the first virtue every person needed to have, but this attitude had begun to decline. Recently the local government in Zhejiang Province established "filial piety to parents" as one of its criteria for promotion of officials, and the national government has legislated that parents have right to sue their children for not visiting them for a long time. Ironically, Confucius's basic morality has to be enforced by law, a practice which he consistently opposed.

In January 2011, a statue of Confucius 9.5 meters tall was placed in Tiananmen Square, sharing the political center of China with his opponent (Mao's portrait is hanging on the gate of the

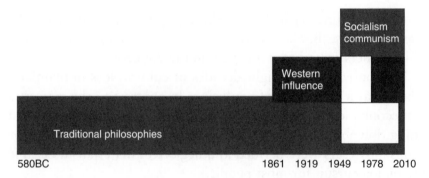

Figure 1.2 *Timeline of the evolution of Chinese culture*

Forbidden City, and his mausoleum is nearby) . Not for nothing is the philosopher, who has survived feudal dynasties and new era revolutions, called "the Master of Eternity." Interestingly, the statue of Confucius was removed to the inside of the national museum on April 20, 2011, the time this book was being completed. This act symbolized the complex attitude of the Chinese towards classical schools of thinking. Figure 1.2 illustrates the evolution of Chinese culture.

SOCIAL STATUS IN MODERN CHINA

Chinese society is ascription-oriented: a person's family background plays a key role. "Where is your family from?" or "What do your parents do?" are the most frequent questions raised during social talk or even a job interview. For some Chinese managers recruiting new staff, family background is more important than education or commercial background. Not surprisingly, "What are your parents' jobs and positions?" is one of the questions in the job application form provided by most Chinese companies. There is an old saying; "The dragon produces a dragon, the Phoenix produces a Phoenix, and the mouse produces a mouse, who is destined to dig a hole." Chinese people are still very class conscious.

Chinese society was classified into four classes by Prime Minister Guanzhong in Qi State, 2,500 years ago. The classes were scholar, farmer, artisan (later, industrial workers) and merchant.

During the Cultural Revolution, Mao recast this to military person, worker, farmer and scholar. This was ruthlessly enforced: "Class struggles" became the daily life of Chinese people. Military people became the upper class, for the first time in Chinese history. Intellectuals suffered particular demotion; they were called "Stinking Number Nine" which means they were the ninth type of people to be abominated, alongside landlord, Kulak, counterrevolutionary, criminal, rightist, betrayer, spy and capitalist-roader.

Deng reinstated the scholar's high status and elevated businesspeople's status enormously. The current social hierarchy is scholar, businessperson, worker, farmer. Although China is the world's fastest growing economy, two thousand years of "scholarship superiority" is still implanted in the Chinese mindset; many entrepreneurs still want their children to become scholars first and then inherit their business as a second choice. As a result, businesspeople classify themselves into a hierarchy of four classes, which are, in descending order of status:

- Official/governmental businesspeople who manage SOEs. Their nickname is "Red Hat Merchant," because the first official businessman in China one and half centuries ago wore a red hat as the symbol of his position. In government, all officials have to be an expert in some academic field or at least have a higher education degree.

- Scholarly businesspeople who have achieved in the academic field and then manage a private business. Their nickname is "Confucian Merchant," as Confucius was the original scholar, and also because these people tend to have a Confucian mindset in leading their business.

- Representatives of foreign companies who are overseas returnees or have trained in multinational corporations (MNCs). Their nickname is "Sea Turtle" (the Chinese phrase for "sea turtle" is pronounced "*haĭ guĭ*," the same as "return from overseas"; this is intended to be teasing rather than dismissive) or "Foreign Comprador."

- Businesspeople from farmer backgrounds, the undereducated entrepreneurs. Most of the first generation of Chinese businesspeople who responded to Deng's call are put in this category. Their nickname is "Peasant Entrepreneur."

CHINESE CULTURAL ATTITUDES TO BUSINESS

As usual with Chinese matters, we begin thousands of years ago, around 4500 BC, when two legendary rulers, Yan and Huang, encouraged business by advocating commodity exchange.

However, when Guanzhong drew up his fourfold characterization of Chinese society, "merchant" was placed at the bottom, below the peasant toiling in his rice field. The great unifying emperor Qin Shihuang similarly disliked commerce, following a "pro-agricultural and anti-commerce" policy advocated by his Legalist mentor Shang Yang. He confined all rich business people to the capital city; he demeaned business people and even sent them to garrison the frontiers alongside criminals. Chinese business and industry stagnated for 2,000 years. The Chinese saying "No businessman trades without fraud" is over a thousand years old, and shows the lack of respect accorded to this section of society for many centuries.

When the British broke down the door of China in 1860 at the end of the Opium Wars, a batch of Chinese intellectuals appealed for a change to the "anti-commerce" mindset, and for strengthening and saving China by boosting commercialization. They proposed adopting the practice of Western capitalism and industrialization. In 1903, the Commerce Ministry was established. Commercial law was enacted. The first generation of national capitalists was born and expected to save China from poverty and the oppression of foreign countries. Most of them were from landlord families and were well educated: the merchant had ascended to second place next to the scholar. However this did not last (in mainland China, anyway): in 1949 Mao, a new Qin Shihuang, came to power. His treatment of the merchant class was as vicious as his treatment of intellectuals.

When Deng took control in 1978, he implemented a "Social market economy with Chinese characteristics." He encouraged common people to pursue individual wealth through a pragmatic approach ("No matter if it's a white cat or a black cat, it is a good cat if it catches mice.") Another phrase of his was "Cross the river by touching the stones," which implied there was no common business practice or culture to follow at that point. Such practice and culture has been developing since then. It has not done so in a straight line, as we have seen. Exactly where it has ended up will be shown in the rest of this book.

2
Leadership Theories

In this chapter, we will look at five leadership theories based on the five main schools of Chinese philosophy.

To some Western readers, this may seem an odd approach. The West doesn't have management theories based on its philosophical traditions, but we do in China. This is partly because of the close relationship that still exists between political and economic power – politicians have always been more prone to place themselves in an intellectual tradition – but mainly because of the powerful effect that these ideas still have in Chinese life.

The Chinese translation of "leadership" is "leading ability," which is a series of strategies and personal skills for managers to equip themselves with. Recently, many Chinese managers have come to believe that they can find prescriptions of leadership in Chinese classical philosophies such as Confucianism, Daoism or Legalism. Mr. Li Dongsheng, the president of TCL (a Chinese Electronic Company) has been quoted as saying, "20 years ago, Chinese entrepreneurs who didn't read Western management books were ignorant, but now those who still read Western management books are incompetent." The justification for this statement is that Chinese philosophies of leadership are richly endowed with practical ideas and common sense.

We will begin with the most influential of the schools, Confucianism.

HUMANE THEORY (CONFUCIANISM)

Confucius's ideal was a harmonious society, where everyone knew their place and role, and fulfilled them. A flavor of his vision can be gathered from this quote of "The Great Harmony" (*dà tóng*) from the *Book of Rites*:

> When the Great Way is practiced, humanity thrives. Those with virtue and ability are chosen and used. People value trustworthiness and cultivate harmony with each other. They treat all old people as their parents, and all children as their children. As a result, the aged have appropriate last years, those in their prime have appropriate employment, and the young have appropriate growth and development. Elderly people with no spouses or children, the handi-capped, and the ill are all provided for... People don't engage in intrigue or trickery, nor do they engage in rob-bery, theft or rebellion. When people leave their houses they don't lock their doors. This is called The Great Harmony.

The same model can be applied to an organization. Figure 2.1 shows the principal tenets of Confucianism and how they are supposed to interact in such an entity.

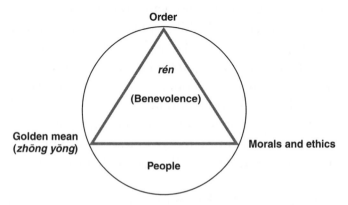

Figure 2.1 *The principle tenets of Confucianism*

To achieve harmony, an organization needs to meet all the criteria indicated in the diagram. This begins with the leader, in the triangle, who needs to practice *"rén"* (benevolence) towards the people, to comply with "order," to apply the golden mean (*"zhōng yōng"*) and to implement a moral and ethical system.

We should look at each of these terms in greater detail.

Rén (Benevolence)

Rén is the key value for the Confucian. A leader should not be a leader if he or she is not *rén* (benevolent). Actually, we should be cautious about the use of the word "benevolent," as there is no perfect literal translation. *Rén* implies a complete code of correct behavior: to show filial piety to parents, to love and respect one's older brothers, to be loyal to the ruler and one's superiors as well as friends. In today's business context, to be *rén* is to be "people-driven," focusing on relationships (including those outside the business sphere), respecting authority and superiors, caring about peers and team members.

This theory requires the leader to be the role model for their organization or team. Such a role model in Confucianism is called *jūnzǐ* (a Person of Honor).

The word *"jūnzǐ"* comprises two Chinese characters. *Jūn* means ruler or husband, but is also a title given to specific honored individuals. *Zi* means "master," a title of respect for a scholar.

In Chinese society to be fully regarded as *jūnzǐ* is a rare attainment. Its combination of erudition, gentleness and active involvement in worldly life is an unusual one. China's former Premier Zhou Enlai is generally regarded as having achieved this status; no other leader from the Communist era has. Yet it is something to which many Chinese aspire, and the nearer you approach this ideal, the greater admiration Chinese people will hold for you.

So, how does one become *jūnzǐ*? In traditional China, people used two metaphors to keep them mindful of the concept: the orchid and the jade. The orchid is elegant, delicate in fragrance and "low profile"; jade is modest, gentle and noble. Growing orchids and wearing a jade pendant was the custom for upper-middle-class men until the collapse of feudalism at the dawn of the twentieth century.

More specifically, to be *jūnzǐ*, a leader needs to:

- Be an intellectual with a comprehensive educational background, capable of constant learning, self-awareness, self-control and self-development.

- Practice filial piety: look after parents and wife, and educate children.

- In conflict, be assertive but not aggressive.

- Be wise, trustworthy, gentle, kind, respectful, frugal and modest.

- Be *rén*, love people properly, be respectful and loyal to authority and superiors, be empathetic to everyone.

- Be fair and just, be responsible and show integrity.

- Follow correct social etiquette in all areas, such as receiving guests, dressing code, table manners.

Order

If a leader has to have the characteristics listed above, their organization has to have the following ones:

Hierarchy

Confucian organizations are very hierarchical, with clear boundaries between each layer.

Confucius said, "If you are not in a certain position, you do not concern yourself with matters concerning that position." This is still a management precept most Chinese accept at work (unlike in the West, where everyone has an opinion on what the people at the top should do).

Because of strict hierarchy, titles are very important. Colleagues call each other "Deputy General Li" rather than "Mr. Li" or the first name. Western business people interacting with Chinese business contacts must make sure they get everybody's titles right, from the first meeting onwards.

It's important to understand that the hierarchy has to be seen by everyone as legitimate. Confucian hierarchy is not just an order imposed on underlings, but one that is accepted by everyone as maximizing the effectiveness of the organization, and thus the common good.

Any attempt to implement a modern "flat" organizational structure would be a challenging task for a Chinese leader, as it flies in the face of the Confucian model. People feel safe in a structured environment.

Relationships

Hierarchies only work if the people in them have "correct" attitudes. Confucius advocated three model relationships to determine principal and subordinate. These were implemented in feudal China for thousands of years and became part of the Chinese mindset. Even in the modern world, it is part of the Chinese subconscious, and can be seen as a "recessive" culture in Chinese organizations.

The three feudal relationships are set out in Table 2.1.

Historically and theoretically, the subordinate should comply with the principal unconditionally. "The King asks his subject to die; the subject must die" was not a myth in Chinese history: in feudal times, many top officials received the death penalty from the Emperor, and accepted it. Of course, the concept has been abused over the centuries by rulers who did not (or chose not to) understand the prerequisite that the principal has to be

Table 2.1 *The three feudal relationships*

Principal	Subordinate
Ruler	Subject
Father	Son
Husband	Wife

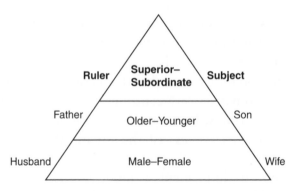

Figure 2.2 *The "psychological contract" in Chinese organizations*

"benevolent-hearted." Confucius did not live to see his ideals abused in this way.

Inherited from this fundamental rule of relationships, there is an underlying "psychological contract" in Chinese organizations, as illustrated in Figure 2.2.

It is still quite common in Chinese organizations for position, age and gender to matter more than actual ability or achievement.

The primacy of the ruler–subject relationship is reflected in the Chinese attitude to authority, which is, by Western standards, deferential. Younger Chinese today may be rebelling against this, but many still accept a higher level of authority than their peers in the West. There is a Chinese saying "Be careful, or the leader will give you tight shoes" (*xiǎo xīn lǐng dǎo gěi nǐ chuān xiǎo xié*). Chinese leaders can make life very difficult for anyone whose challenge becomes uncomfortable to them. People in China are used to living in the shadow of being given tight shoes.

The relationship between father (parent) and son (child) also has immense power in Chinese life. The relationship was more complex and subtle than is often thought: an unequal role did not mean unequal obligations. Yes, the child's obligation was more powerful, but the parents owed affection, sustenance, respect and self-sacrifice to their children. Here is a traditional Chinese tale we were taught as children:

A warrior leaves his pregnant wife to fight for his emperor, and returns home after 20 years. As he nears his home he sees a young archer shooting at a wild pig and they get talking. This is, of course, his son, but neither of them realizes this. The young man challenges him to an archery contest and accidentally the young man is killed.

In this tale, one person has committed two cardinal sins. Who?

Westerners to whom we tell this story come up with different answers. Some say the father, for deserting his wife, for failing to inform his wife he was coming home after 20 years and just expecting everyone to recognize him, or just for being such a lousy shot that he kills a fellow participant in an archery contest. (Silly old fool – he ought to know when his time is up and get out of the way of the younger, fitter man!) Others say the lad, for being a show-off and running unnecessary risk. A third group blames the mother, for not teaching the son enough about his father so that the boy did not recognize him when he appeared. And I've even had "the emperor" as a reply, for taking a father away from his pregnant wife. No Chinese would doubt the answer for a moment. It is, of course, the son, because he (a) did not know his father and (b) challenged his father.

The Confucian husband–wife relationship has often been misunderstood as a kind of charter for exploitation. This is not entirely the case. The three relationships always involve reciprocal respect, duties and joint submission to higher, collective goals. Many Chinese women are powerful individuals, often behind the scenes but not always. Empress Wu Zetian ruled China very efficiently during the Tang dynasty. In modern China women hold many senior positions, but it could be said not in sufficient numbers.

The prejudice against females is still very subtle but pervasive. Yet things are better than they were, at least partially thanks to Mao who encouraged Chinese women to go to work and provided equal opportunity in education and the workplace. However, he had thousands of years of tradition to fight against. Confucius didn't exactly help either, though: Confucian scholars work hard to put a nonsexist gloss on some of his utterances like "Women and small men are difficult to deal with." The perception of "male superiority" still haunts China: the "glass ceiling" exists everywhere in organizations and government, a true "elephant in the room." Some of the few women at the top in government are dismissively nicknamed "Innocent Maidens" (*wú zhī shào nǚ*). This is a typically Chinese pun: the words sound similar to the words for "Nonparty, Intellectual, Minority and Female," a Chinese version of affirmative action. This is one of the major differences between China and the West: Chinese women don't perceive "Innocent Maiden" as a "dismissive" name, rather, we see it just as a tease. Probably, that is why we don't have the Western concept feminist.

The Golden Mean (zhōng yōng)

"*Zhōng*" means moderate, right, impartial; "*yōng*" means normal, ordinary and amiable. Confucius believed that *zhōng yōng* is the best way to manage any organization, it is the true art of leadership. It is not something that can be acquired by formal training – it is the result of self-cultivation. Exactly how you achieve it is not clearly set out. (If this is beginning to sound mysteriously "Oriental," here's a quote from Warren Bennis that could have come straight out of the *Analects*: "Leadership is difficult to define. It is like beauty, hard to describe but you know it when you see it.")

The following key points may reveal some hints:

- Never be extreme (not too much, not too little). Never take extreme action; instead, find a way in between. Find the solution that all parties can accept and where all parties benefit.

- Be yourself, collaborate but do not compromise your values and beliefs.

- Establish *guānxì* (connection) with others. *Guānxì* are the informal but powerful relationships from which networks are built up in China. Normally, you initiate *guānxì* with someone through mutual friends or acquaintances who are trusted by both parties: in China it takes time to instill trust. *Guānxì* is widely accepted as the way, the "*dào*," to do business in China.

- Be flexible, fitting in with changing situations.

- Be astute; adapt your style to circumstances.

- Manage conflict; collaborate with all parties impartially and resolve things unobtrusively.

Because there is no clear manual to follow – ultimately, *zhōng yōng* is about personal development – many Chinese leaders fall short of its requirements. Common failings include:

- Over-compromising, leading to giving up your own standpoints, and resulting in "you win, I lose."

- Giving up principles to please others.

- Changing all the time to suit a superior.

- Loss of direction and focus.

- Political maneuvering.

- Abuse of *guānxì* for personal gain.

Morals and Ethics
Confucians believe that people are naturally born good, so in order to make an organization sustainable the leader should implement a moral and ethical system, rather than rules. People within that organization should be educated, but not forced, to be aware of self-control, self-improvement and what they should not do. There would be no punishment if they did wrong, but help for them to change attitude.

This is something of an ideal – it would only work if everyone was, or at least aspired to be, *jūnzǐ*.

Confucius's distrust of legal compulsion explains why Westerners often consider that Chinese lack a sense of legal responsibility.
A contract, such Westerners say, is just seen as a piece of paper,
not something that has to be followed. In the period of China's
reopening from the mid 1980s to the mid 1990s, there were many
accusations of fraud leveled at Chinese business people by foreign business partners. In many cases, the accused were not really
aware of their legal responsibility.

Harmony

Putting the above precepts into practice should produce harmony, which is the optimal state for Chinese society and any
Chinese organization (and has been for thousands of years). The
Chinese word for harmony comprises two characters, *hé xié*. *Hé*
means peace, moderation and reconciliation; *xié* means coordi-
nation and congruence. A harmonious organization effects the
unity of opposites; it is a place where different people get on,
where disagreements are discussed openly but politely in a search
for common ground. It balances competing and accommodating, strictness and tolerance, *yīn* and *yáng*. In it, people give
of their best because they are respected, believe in the common
good and are given the right jobs so they do what they are
best at.

To visualize harmony, look at traditional Chinese paintings. The
aim is to balance four elements, human, landscape, plants and animal, and create a feeling of calm, joy, peace, balance, relaxation
and happiness. You will be released from strong emotions.

Mottoes such as "*hé wéi guì*" ("harmony is most precious") and
"*jiā hé wàn shì xīng*" ("a family that lives in harmony will prosper") are the ones that Chinese leaders value most in business.
It is this thinking that led President Hu to launch the "Harmonious Society" in China, as China is in transition; growing fast,
and experiencing drastic changes. Stability and solidarity, rather
than change and profit, remain the priority for Chinese leaders,
particularly at SOEs.

Here are some signs of a harmonious Confucian organization:

- A focus on training and personal development.

- A strong ethical sense. People interact with each other with conscious understanding of ethics and respect for position. There is little need for formal regulation.

- Hierarchy. A centralized organization with a hierarchy that everyone understands and accepts.

- A Person of Honor "*jūn zǐ*" as leader. This person is "*rén*," and is a role model that others follow. Such a leader will have missions to improve him or herself and to manage the organization, which they see as a kind of family. They may also aspire to political power, which they will seek in order to do good both for the country and the world.

- Honor extends through the hierarchy. All middle management and above are refined intellectuals who are superior in morality, intelligence, interpersonal skills, self-discipline, modesty and good taste. Like the leader, they act as role models.

- Ethics extending beyond work – especially to families. Employees will be "family people" and the organization will respect and encourage this.

It is understood that this is an ideal. Short-term pressures can militate against this ideal. Even the most well-meaning leaders will find themselves trying to balance harmony against the needs of day-to-day business.

Humane Theory is probably the one most accepted by Chinese leaders as well as by the majority of employees who work for SOEs. It fits other Chinese values such as face, the importance of relationships and job security. However, its rigidity, bureaucracy, and incomplete institutional system also constrain the development of organizations.

We will now move on to look at alternative models. Remember that the *Yi Jing* insists that no human model is absolutely right, and that different models can be applied in different situations.

So these other models are not incompatible "rivals" but simply other clubs in the Chinese leadership golf-bag.

ALTRUISTIC THEORY (MOHISM)

Mo Zi established "ten creeds" which we have, for business purposes, consolidated into six, and which are represented in Figure 2.3.

- Paternalistic dictatorship. A leader is to be a great person and worshiped in the organization. He or she must be wise, strong and kind; he or she must set up the goal for his team and protect them if things get difficult. He or she must be the one who controls their own destiny.

- Employee benefit. It is the key pursuit of the leader to satisfy employees' basic needs. Mutual benefit is critical.

- Fraternal team. People care about each other and take others' interests as priority. Teams are brotherhood clubs.

- Minimum cost. Keep costs low, for yourself and for your employees, whom you encourage by example to lead a simple, unadorned life without desires beyond basic needs.

- Reward and punishment. Set up clear and rigorous procedures for employees to follow, and serious punishment for noncompliance.

- Peaceful coexistence with competitors. Initiate peace with competitors by noninterference and respect for their autonomy.

Mohism is a theory for tough times, when everyone has to pull together and there's not a lot to go round. Mao Zedong can be seen as a master Mohist. In the past, many advocates of Mohism turned to follow Confucianism as soon as times became more pleasant – as has China after 1978. Yet Mao's

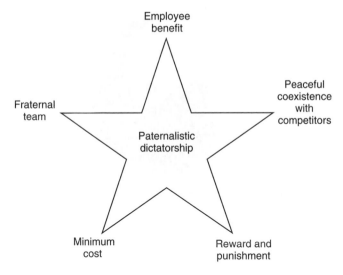

Figure 2.3 *Creeds of Altruistic Theory*

Mohist legacy lives on, especially in manufacturing industry in less Western-influenced parts of the country.

Everyone can learn some lessons from this philosophy. The leader needs to understand junior employees, who are likely to be not well-educated, especially if they come from poor families. If such people are ignored, in a rush of enthusiasm for Confucian high-mindedness, they may feel resentment and damage the culture of the organization. As an old, and rather cynical, Chinese saying has it, "the environment at home is determined by the person who earns most, and the cultural environment is determined by the person who is educated least."

NATURALISTIC THEORY (DAOISM)

Harmony

In Humane Theory, harmony is created by the leader; in Naturalistic Theory it is driven by a dynamic of environment and people. The organization is a constantly changing organism in which all parties are inextricably intertwined; harmony is kept by maintaining the balance of *yīn* and *yáng* (in Figure 2.4, the white part is *yáng*, the dark part is *yīn*). The underlying change is

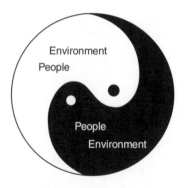

Figure 2.4 *Naturalistic Theory (Daoism)*

not controllable: the organization and its people need to adjust themselves and adapt to these powerful, essentially mysterious underlying forces.

In an organization that operates by the Daoist principles of Naturalistic Theory:

- The organizational structure is decentralized and flat.

- The leader is invisible and is an aptly summed up by a quote attributed to Lao Zi about leadership style:

    As for the best leaders . . . the people do not notice their existence.
    The next best . . . the people honor and praise.
    The next . . . the people fear.
    And the next . . . the people hate.
    When the best leader's work is done, the people say "We did it ourselves."

- Each department has great autonomy.

- There is little communication between functions.

- Long-term policy remains fixed, with minimum changes.

- Comfortable living is the final goal for organization as well as employees.

- The organization minimizes interaction with the external environment.

- There will be as low a level of technology as possible. This simplicity prevents competition over resources.

- The workplace will be healthy but not entertaining.

- The organization keeps a low profile in public.

- Employees are well looked after in terms of welfare but not career development.

Environment

This can be timing, place, government policy, international dynamics – anything that is not directly controlled by the people in the organization. The environment is the primary factor, and it can be predicted but not controlled. The role of a leader is to understand and predict environmental change and find the best possible environment for organization to perform.

People

The ideal employee is not ambitious, flexible, adaptable, unsophisticated. If they are not well-educated, even better.

The following characters are needed for the leader:

- Be calm.

- Be reactive, not "proactive."

- Implement stable policy systematically to avoid drastic changes.

- Focus on people's well-being and organizational stability but not their personal development.

- Laissez-faire: invisible leading – empower and delegate.

- Be less ambitious both for self and the organization

- Be low-key, modest, industrious and frugal

- Show some degree of weakness, fragility and stupidity, as a normal person.

- Have a sense of crisis, be prepared for danger in times of safety.

- Be like water: mild, flexible, adaptable, tolerant, accommodating and persistent.

- Believe that "no-one will fight the one who does not fight."

- In all things, seek balance, the unity of opposites, Yīn and Yáng; for example work–life balance.

Daoism believes that a leader who acts as above will realize "*Dào*" and maintain harmony in all aspects – which will make the organization sustainable. This theory has its advantage in areas where there is little competition or in slow-growing markets.

Some Chinese leaders of small and medium companies in second- or third-tier cities practice this theory, and it does work for them in those environments – to some extent, anyway. However, the Daoist dream, of a "small country with little population," where people live equally and happily, with no competition or materialistic temptations, is a Shangri-la. Such conditions have never prevailed in history. A number of emperors and scholars have in the past given up their power and extravagant life to pursue Naturalism – and have suffered accordingly. Perhaps David Cameron may find this theory useful for his "well-being index"!

Fundamentally, China is, and always has been, a power-driven, high power-distance society,[1] where ascending the organizational and social hierarchy is the primary pursuit for the majority. The

---

[1] In high power-distance cultures, people are more likely to accept great differences in a company hierarchy where power is spread unequally; also authority will be more concentrated and centralized in a high power-distance organization. In low power-distance cultures, people are unlikely to accept the concentration of power, the organization is more decentralized, and managers will tend to develop closer relationships with their subordinates; also, in such cultures, power tends to be subjected to variety of laws, procedures and standards.

statue of Confucius in Tiananmen Square will encourage even more people to strive for official careers in government, following the Sage's advice: "He who excels in study can follow an official career." The power of top officials in business and government will increase. Don't expect a statue of Lao Zi to appear in Tiananmen Square any time soon!

The twin concepts of *yīn* and *yáng* both figure in the oldest books of Chinese, the Book of Odes (*Shi Jing*) and Book of Changes (*Yi Jing*, better known in the West as the *I Ching*). The latter is supposed to be over 4,000 years old.

The *yīn–yáng* theory is the most characteristic and pervasive concept in Chinese thinking. The literal meanings of *yīn* and *yáng* are the shadowy and sunny sides of a hill, and so, by extension, darkness and light. *Yīn–yáng* represents all the opposing principles we find in the universe. Thus, under *yáng* we have the principles of sun, heaven, maleness and dominance, while under *yīn* we have the principle of cold, darkness, femaleness and submission. Each of these opposites produces the other, so that everything in the world is a mixture of the two: though there is in one sense a struggle between these elements, the struggle is transcended by their interdependence.

Western logic finds it harder than the Chinese to deal with the perpetual coexistence of opposites. This tolerance of duality affects the way that the Chinese think about business. In negotiations, for example, Chinese thinking would be based on trying to find a situation whereby the outcome would be X *and* Y (a win–win outcome) and not X *or* Y (the zero-sum game all negotiators seek to avoid). This partially explains the protracted negotiation process you will encounter in China.

The *Yi Jing* (*I Ching*) is an immensely powerful book. It is still popular – and used – in modern China, where there is a *Yi Jing* association and a number of *Yi Jing* masters whose advice is in great demand.

INSTITUTIONAL THEORY (LEGALISM)

Legalism applied in the business context becomes Institutional Theory. Legalism emphasizes three things: authority, law (regulation) and tactics (management techniques) – in that order of importance, as illustrated in Figure 2.5.

This theory would suit anyone interested in corporate governance, as it insists on strict and transparent regulations as well as justice and equality: to the Legalist, "everyone is equal before the law."

Looking at these three levels in more detail:

- *Authority*: Legalist leaders must lead and be seen to lead. Everyone knows who's boss.

- *Regulation*: Establish comprehensive and workable regulations and ensure employees follow them rigorously and consistently.

- *Management techniques*:

    o   Set up a profit-driven culture.

    o   Articulate everyone's job description. Make sure there are no overlapping duties and that people are only allowed to do what is outlined in their contract.

    o   Manage people by satisfying their self-interest with clear targets.

    o   Conduct scrupulous performance appraisal, focusing on tangible outcomes.

    o   Cautiously promote people to higher positions.

    o   Be rational and fair to everyone, regardless of position.

It can be seen that this is almost the opposite of Humane Theory (though Daoists might disagree, if they could be bothered). Yet both are respected in Chinese organizational life. The tension between them makes things difficult for Chinese managers, who

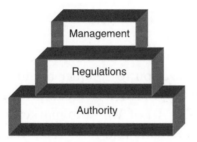

Figure 2.5 *The structure of Institutional Theory*

often want to run things in a more Legalist manner, but find the Confucian pressure of personal relationships preventing this.

In the mid 1990s, the Chinese government launched the concept of the "Legal Society" to educate people into legal consciousness. A number of legal cases were brought, where employers had been using the old "moral" mindset, and violated the law by engaging in fraud or physically punishing employees. Recently Chinese SOEs have launched "scientific management" schemes, aiming to learn from the West in order to improve operational efficiency. Some of this maps well on to Legalism.

However, the dominant culture in Chinese businesses, especially SOEs, remains Confucian and Humane. Institutional theory remains just that, a theory, happily discussed by armchair experts in the comfort of their club.

Redundancy remains a huge headache for essentially Confucian SOEs. And the senior SOE manager who makes a serious mistake will still stay at the same management level, though may possibly be transferred to another business unit. In a private company or a JV (Joint Venture), Institutional theory is more likely to prevail, but even here, Chinese mangers are still reluctant to sack people.

The reality is that Chinese managers find themselves torn between the twin pressures of Confucian harmony and profit. Balancing these two desirables is their most challenging task.

STRATEGIC THEORY (MILITARISM)

The founders of Militarism defined Strategic Theory as "how commanders lead the army to battle against the enemy, taking

advantage of situational contingences in order to win victories."
(Chen and Lee, 2008).

In business, we will define the leader as a strategist, whose aim
is to lead the organization to conquer the market. Marketers, in
particular, love this approach: it is not surprising that Philip Kotler
transformed Sun Zi's *Art of War* into marketing strategy.

The theory is pragmatic and moderate. While the objective is
to conquer the market, all-out war is best avoided: a strategic
alliance is better than destructive competition.

To be a strategic leader, you need to see the big picture. This is
done by looking at four perspectives as shown in Figure 2.6.

Looking at these in a little more detail:

- *Strategy*: Have the skill to use unorthodox strategies. Be wise,
  trustworthy, benevolent, courageous, assertive, flexible and
  adaptable.

- *Regulation*: Focus on process with a "marketing-oriented"
  mindset. Implement scientific management systems with suc-
  cinct and clear rules and policies. Implement clear and fair
  reward and punishment schemes equally at all levels – but at
  the same time temper this with a dose of pragmatism.

- *People*: Build high-morale teams that are "goal-driven." Delegate to team leaders who make decisions in their own business
  units. Be sociable and proactive, networking both inside and
  outside the organization.

- *Situation*: Always be aware of the changing environment.
  Adapt to it, or, even better, leverage it proactively to put the
  odds in your favor.

This theory neatly bridges Humane Theory and Institutional Theory, and is thus more pleasant for people to accept. However, it
relies on the leader being a brilliant strategist, both in dealing
with the world out there and in dealing with internal issues. Such
people are few and far between.

Table 2.2 summarizes all of the different leadership schools. The
"Key points" listed in the table are also the key Chinese values.

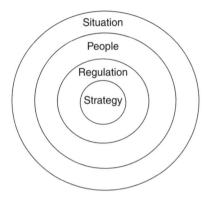

Figure 2.6 *The approach of Strategic Theory*

Table 2.2 *Schools of leadership in summary*

Leadership Theory	Philosophical School	Key points
Humane Theory	Confucianism	• Create a harmonious organization • Follow the order of hierarchy and relationship • Leader as *jūnzǐ*, *rén*, benevolent-hearted • Lead by morals and ethics with the Golden Mean (*zhōng yōng*) • People-driven • Focus on employee education • Role-modeling • Self-cultivation
Altruistic Theory	Mohism	• Paternalistic dictatorship • Focus on employee benefit • Fraternal teamwork • Reward and punishment • Self-sacrifice
Naturalistic Theory	Daoism	• Following the harmonious environment • Invisible leader, laissez-faire • Focus on employee welfare

Table 2.2 *(Continued)*

Leadership Theory	Philosophical School	Key points
		• Leader as water: mild, tolerant, benevolent, persistent • Work–life balance • Self-realization
Institutional Theory	Legalism	• Authority • Rigorous and consistent regulation • Task-driven • Focus on employee interest • Self-discipline
Strategic Theory	Militarism	• Strategy-oriented • Scientific management system • Goal-directed • Focus on team morale • Situation awareness • Self-motivation

It is worth noting that word "leader" in China is classified at two levels, each with its own name. A first-level leader is called "*lǐng xiù*," which means literally "collar and sleeve," a name derived by analogy from ancient Chinese customs of dress – collar and sleeve were the parts of a costume that distinguished the most important people . *Lǐng xiù* are mainly political leaders, in charge of country, party, society and religion. A second-level leader is called "*lǐng dǎo*" ("lead and guide"). These are people at the executive level in organizations. In this book we focus on the second-level leadership, "lead and guide."

3
Core Chinese Cultural Features

Chapters 1 and 2 gave us a brief outline of the philosophical and cultural foundations of Chinese leadership. The aim of this chapter is to provide an introduction to some of the core features of Chinese society. These are, of course, developed from the traditions we have been looking at, but have since entered Chinese life to such an extent that they lie at the heart of the thoughts, emotions, beliefs, values, judgments and actions of all Chinese people, even if they have never read a word that Confucius or Lao Zi ever wrote.

We could write an entire book – or several, actually – about these matters, but to keep our message brief we will focus on the three cultural features that we consider to be the most essential to grasp: face, *guānxì* and harmony.

These three concepts are intimately linked and related.

FACE

There is no record in Chinese history of how "face" became one of the Chinese core cultural features, but by the time of Confucius it had become of enormous importance.

It has remained so ever since. Face is like DNA, it's "in the Chinese blood." It is an "invisible hand" that controls Chinese people's attitudes and behavior at all times. An old saying is that face is "more important than Heaven," another is that a person would rather die than lose face.

The concept is a complex one. The Western notion of "face," as in the phrases "losing face" or "saving face," partially covers it, but in a rather watered-down way. It can be interpreted as self-respect, respect for others, creating a harmonious environment, building good relationships and concern about one's standing in the group.

You must give everyone face whatever you do. It is one of the core cultural features of the Chinese people and is a key component in the dynamics of *guānxì* (connections) which we will cover later.

Westerners often wonder why the Chinese make such a fuss about face. Doesn't everyone have some sense of dignity that can get hurt at an insult? To take such a line is understandable – especially when you have just strayed over some line of Chinese etiquette that makes no sense to you – but is very dangerous. Face matters in China the way that it just doesn't in the West. It is not just about feelings, but a key part of what holds society together. There are numerous examples of people losing power, or friendships destroyed, over face. Carl Crow, a writer on China in early 1930s, understood this concept and its importance:

> No-one in China is too lowly to treasure and guard his "face," that is his dignity and self-respect. And no foreign resident has ever accomplished anything in dealing with Chinese if he failed to take this factor into account. Those who know how to utilize it have found life pleasant and sometimes prosperous. (Crow, 1937)

Here are some key pointers about this powerful concept:

- It's a dynamic concept. One can receive, lose or save face. Many Westerners seem to understand this quite well conceptually, but the actual mechanics of how these things happen remain totally unclear to them. Face is so important that it justifies spending money even if you have little of it. Good examples are people who entertain lavishly at expensive restaurants even when they cannot afford it, and new businesses that rent prestigious, expensive premises in apparently inappropriate locations.

- Face is more to do with one's social role rather than about oneself. Many Westerners will look at the above examples and think the Chinese person involved is simply showing off. They might say that person has a "big ego." But this is totally to misinterpret what is going on. At the same time as "bigging up" their importance socially, the person will remain undemonstrative about themselves as an individual. In China, individuals count for nothing on their own. Individuals are always expected to be humble about themselves. But they are allowed to be forceful about their social roles. This key distinction seems hypocritical to Westerners, but it must be understood in order to make progress in Chinese society.

- Face not only applies to individuals but also to organizations and countries. Chinese ministries and corporations have face to keep, which is a major reason why government officials used to ride in big Soviet limousines with the curtains drawn and now tend to prefer Audi A8 cars. The Chinese government went to every length possible to ensure that the 2008 Olympics and Shanghai Expo 2010 turned out to be the most successful ever – and most of the world agreed that they succeeded.

- Face is intimately connected to the concept of *guānxì*, which we will talk about below. Loss of face means reduced social resources to use in cultivating and developing one's connection network. Face is gained by good connections, wealth, power and intelligence.

- Face can be likened to a credit card: the more you have in the account, the more credit you are given. But you can extend this too far, "overdraw on your face" and find yourself in debt. In the long run, the face account needs to be in balance. One can lose face unwittingly as illustrated in Figure 3.1.

Looking at the dynamics of face in greater detail:
How does one lose face? Figure 3.1 summarizes this.

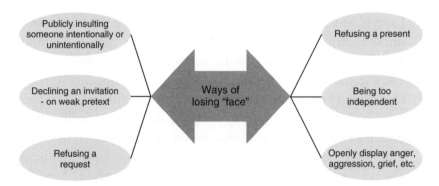

Figure 3.1 *Ways of losing face*

- Publicly insulting someone intentionally, or even unintentionally, is an affront to one's own personal dignity (as it upsets harmony) as well as an insult to the dignity of the victim. So face is lost all round.

  The unintentional aspect is particularly difficult for outsiders. "We don't know these complex rules: how can we be blamed for getting them wrong from time to time?" Answer: because you're in China, and these rules apply here. We have seen this happen time and time again. A recent example was during a banquet given by the foreign participant in a Joint Venture. The president of the foreign partner made a well-crafted speech, full of praise for his Chinese counterparts, then everyone proceeded to have dinner. The Chinese were greatly offended: the president of the Chinese partner had not been invited to make a speech, too. As a result, face was lost all round: for the Chinese president who did not get to speak, but also for the Western president who did not have the sophistication, insight or consideration to invite him.

- Declining an invitation to a social or business function on a weak pretext. Sometimes, people find themselves in the difficult position of being invited to clashing engagements. Recently, a very successful Hong Kong businessman we know was invited to three dinner engagements on the same night.

In the West, he would probably have either accepted the first invitation, telling the others "I'm sorry, but I'm already busy that evening" or made up some excuse and gone to the most important one. Neither of these strategies were available to the Hong Kong businessman, however: he had to attend all three parties, spending less time at each party but both "giving face" to all his hosts and preserving his own face too.

- Refusing a request. This can seem a minefield for outsiders – it seems like another fiendish oriental way for putting foreigners at a disadvantage and getting them to do things for nothing. "What, you mean I have to do everything I'm asked? I'm busy!"

  If it's any consolation, Chinese find this difficult too. However there is strict etiquette in China around this rule. The first point is simply that it is not done to ask for extravagant favors from people, because you put them in a position of having to grant them or lose face. Another is the principle of *guānxì*: the closer connections you have to someone, the bigger favor you can ask. This is why trust takes time to build: one aspect of being trusted is that the other person knows you will only ask for reasonable favors or, if you do ask for something big, it will be because you are in truly dire need.

- Refusing a present. The sender will lose a lot of face in this situation, feeling perhaps that their present is not good enough and also feeling that he/she is looked down upon by the receiver. Accepting presents gives face to the sender and saves your own face.

- Being too independent. When you are having a meal at a restaurant and one party offers to pay for the meal, under Chinese etiquette it is appropriate to offer to pay too. You then haggle as to who should pay: in the end, your Chinese host should "win" and pay. Foreigners often find this confusing: used to perhaps one round of haggling back home, they start wondering if they really should pay after all. In reality, you just have to play the game. What you should not do is offer to "go Dutch." This would be construed as not giving face to the person who offered to pay, perhaps even indicating you don't want to be close to them, or even an insult, implying that your host cares so much about a little money. Loss of face all round!

- Expressing emotions uncontrollably leads to loss of face. This extends to all emotions. In the West, anger and aggression can sometimes be seen as the style of a good manager – "X is abrasive, but he gets things done." This is not true in China. X is seen as crude, lacking in self-discipline and unworthy of respect, and his successes will turn out to be short-term. Even grief, an emotion Westerners not only accept but consider it strange if someone does not show it, falls into this category. Emotion is out, period.

  Many an expatriate manager has shown anger and aggression – and even grief – in the Chinese workplace. The result is that their Chinese staff will disengage from the now-shamed manager, who ultimately loses control and authority.

If face has been damaged, what do you do?

We regret to have to tell you it's a long haul. Third parties or intermediaries are used in both business and personal situations. Recently, one of the writers inadvertently offended one of his Chinese friends and had to ask a mutual friend to find out why the friend was cool to the writer's overtures to socialize. Only then was the writer able to find out what had happened and apologize. Even so, the relationship is not back to where it was: The writer will have put work in to develop it again. (So take courage from this story: this happens all the time between Chinese – as a foreigner you may consider yourself adrift in a sea in which everyone else is happily sailing along, but this is not the case.)

One thing you cannot do is give yourself face – it has to be given by others.

Yet you can behave in certain ways that will bring it about, that people will start according face to you. If there were a word to sum up the right kind of behavior to gain face, it would be "diplomatic." Here are some pointers

- Position yourself in a social context so that your Chinese hosts can understand you, by demonstrating you are part of a network.

- When you meet, give details of your job position and company. Giving your business card when you first meet a Chinese businessperson is essential. Make sure this card has a title on it – "Vice-President, Sales" – something Western cards sometimes omit in the attempt to appear pally and informal. Chinese will just think you are a nobody! And remember to both give and receive name cards with both hands, which is also a way to show face.

- Use people's titles correctly. It could be said that people who don't have enough self-confidence tend to be obsessed with face, and overreact in some circumstances. For instance, some people can be very upset and perceive they are losing face if their titles are not used correctly, such as Professor X or General Manager Y.

- Give details of people you know. In the West this can be construed as "name dropping": in China it gives both you and your interlocutor face.

- When meeting people for the first time, establish some common ground both socially and professionally.

- Ask about the other person and discover more about them. In a group setting, the smart, face-earning person notes some fact about every individual, and leaves with a comment to each about that fact, thus giving them all face and getting face for themselves too.

To gain face requires a high level of personal development in terms of values, beliefs, attitude and behavior. The person who is recognized as a real "face-holder" is seen as highly authentic.

In reality, very few people have this high level of face – people who can dedicate themselves to ongoing and nonstop self development and help others develop at the same time too.

If this all sounds unrealistically high-minded, it is also true that a less admirable version of face is simply coterminous with authority. Authority is highly respected in China, and many people have automatic face because of their official position.

Western readers may wonder if this is also true for women in China. It all sounds very male to me!

As we have said, face is very much connected with the notion of guānxì, which we now turn to.

GUĀNXÌ

There are so many definitions of *guānxì* that there is a danger of confusing the fundamental essence of what it really stands for. One translation is "relationships." More subtly, it consists of connections defined by reciprocity, trust and mutual obligation; in other words, friendship with implications of a continual exchange of favors.

Etymologically, *guān* is a derivative word meaning "door" or "pass," while *xì* is a very old word with connotations of hierarchy (a point we owe to Tim Ambler of London Business School). Therefore, the term literally means "door into a hierarchy or group." You are either on the right side of the door or the wrong side of it!

Guānxì is the platform for social and business activities in China. It can be seen as the *"dào"* which drives all dynamics. If you heard "Do you have *dào*?" in a Chinese conversation (it is quite a common question), it means "Do you have *guānxì*?" Build up your *guānxì* and be aware of the dynamic of *guānxì* around you before you do anything.

Guānxì exists in four forms, based on the closeness of a relationship. These are (in descending order of importance):

- *Jiārén*: Consists of family members. Despite the one-child policy, Chinese families are more extended than Western ones. Nonfamily can be co-opted into this network, but it is rare.

- *Zìjǐrén*: A small group of really close friends. They say "you can count your true friends on the fingers of one hand": these are very special people with whom no favor is too much.

- *Shúrén*: These are more distant friends or colleagues. Usually there is some long-standing or formal tie. *Shúrén* often come from the same village or area (this means much more to Chinese than to Westerners) or are fellow-members of societies (the Chinese love forming and joining societies, especially from school and college days). You will have a lot of links in common.

- *Shengren*: These are outsiders, who look as if they might be useful contacts (or good friends) but about whom this judgment has not yet been made. Such a judgment can take a long time, as Westerners eager to get to China and "get on with stuff" soon find out. As you get older, you tend to have fewer *shēngrén guānxì*: either you know and trust people, so they are in one of the top three categories above, or they are just acquaintances and thus outside the "*guānxì wǎng*" (the network).

The first three categories are unlikely (for most Chinese) to include Westerners: the fourth category may well include some.

How Do You Attain *guānxì*?

There are a number of ways in which foreigners improve their chances of acquiring *guānxì*, even up to the level of *shúrén*:

- A Chinese husband or wife. You are now caught up in the net of family obligations that is Chinese society. There are now people who can be shamed if you do not deliver on a promise.

- You speak perfect Chinese. This does seem to elevate foreigners to the position of "honorary Chinese" even though you still have the ability to leave China and never come back. Perfect Chinese implies you have committed time and effort to the study of China and its ways, as well as meaning you can participate in conversations at all levels.

- You are a "friend of China." For many years after his diplomatic drive to open China to the West in the early 1970s, Henry Kissinger was used extensively by foreign companies to open doors in China. The Chinese remember such gestures and retain long-term bonds with such people. Clearly we cannot all be Henry Kissinger, but there are smaller-scale benefits foreigners can bring to China which will be valued by your local hosts.

Advice on *guānxì*

It still looks hard for an ordinary Western manager to qualify for the necessary *guānxì*. We make some comments:

- Foreigners can develop what we call "probational *guānxì*" quite quickly. As we said above, the very fact of your being part of a business that is working in China implies you are at least beginning to fall into the "friend of China" category, and the longer you stay in China (and the more resources your business is seen to be committing to it), the stronger this will become. In practice, you will begin to form alliances the moment you arrive, and these are best treated as if you are developing formal *guānxì* – which may end up happening. Hence our term "probational *guānxì*."

  When you arrive, and are seen to be of some importance, you will be invited to enter individuals' networks. The Chinese work very hard to cultivate new friends: most foreigners in China are targeted quite hard, as they are perceived to be well connected and wealthy. Is this cynicism on behalf of the Chinese? By idealistic standards the answer must be yes. But be more subtle: a wise view is to admit that the Chinese have a strong vein of pragmatism in how they form and maintain relationships, but at the same time people can and do form friendships.

In practice, Chinese people place foreigners in three categories. Working upwards, we begin with people with whom we have no real plan to form a relationship. A tourist visiting China would be an example of this, or a journalist who takes a very anti-Chinese view of things. Second are people with whom it is expedient to build a relationship, but who are not respected. Examples of this category would be the classic expatriate manager who spends all his or her time in a special foreigners' compound, moaning about China and counting the days till his or her next placement. Such a person needs to be dealt with, but will only receive superficial politeness. The third category is the foreigner who is both perceived as important politically (in the broadest sense of the word) and respected.

To place oneself in this third category should be the aim of everybody seeking to manage a Chinese team successfully. And such a person will find themselves making real steps onto the *guānxì* ladder.

- The more you are perceived as thinking like a Chinese person, the more quickly you will be welcomed into real *guānxì* networks.

- Introductions are a huge part of *guānxì* dynamics. Westerners often ask Chinese for introductions without understanding what this involves. If we introduce you to people in our *guānxì* network, that places an obligation on them to put themselves out for us. They are only doing it because of us – they don't know you. In return, we will have to do them a favor later. Furthermore, favors will probably be unequal to start with. You, a newcomer, have little to offer the important dealmaker who sets things up for you. But the system is long term. The expectation is that over time you will repay him or her with favors.

Figure 3.2 illustrates some of the ways one can develop and maintain *guānxì*.

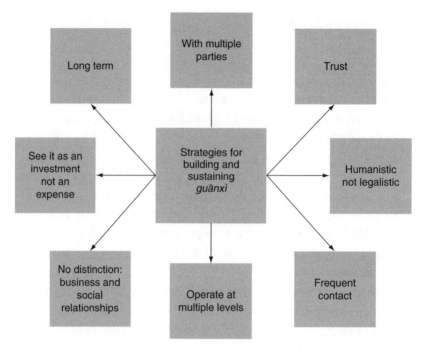

Figure 3.2 *Strategies for building and sustaining* guānxì

Some comments on Figure 3.2:

- Developing *guānxì* occurs in stages and involves a lot of time. This can vary from a few months to years: you have to be in this for the long term. It should be seen as an investment rather than an expense because if you are well connected, this confers access to resources, people and information that you can then leverage.

- Trust is an unwritten code of business in China: normally if a person does not trust you they are unlikely to do business.

- Remember that the basis of *guānxì* is human dynamics – by implication it involves reciprocity from each party. To maintain *guānxì*, it is really necessary to keep frequent contacts, face to face and outside business hours. There must be consistent communications and invitations to golf, dinner, cultural events. At some stage you may be asked to help with nonbusiness favors: building *guānxì* recognizes no distinction between the professional and private spheres of life, and therefore operates at multiple levels.

Guānxì and the Modern Business Context

China's economy has developed rapidly over the last 30 years, but the same cannot be said of its institutional frameworks: the laws and regulations governing business remain somewhat chaotic and not easily accessible for all to see. Also, central and local government remained key actors on the economic stage. Government officials are still important conduits for understanding the regulatory system and for other necessary information such as getting licenses, procedures to obtain permits and other necessary pieces of official business.

It is in this context that businesses turned to personal relationships to act as a catalyst or lubricant to get things done in China by opening doors to resources and information, but in a way that remains above board and legal. *Guānxì* circumvents or neutralizes the bureaucratic system. It may even be said that *guānxì* with government officials is perhaps more important than *guānxì* with other managers or nongovernment business contacts, because of the centrality of the State in the Chinese economy. With the right *guānxì*, there are few rules in China that can't be broken or at least bent: We have heard *guānxì* described as "a tool to achieve the impossible."

Socially and individually, people in China also have little confidence or trust in the legal/regulatory system and prefer to trust their personal relationships. *Guānxì* assumes some of the functions of a legal system – "mutual favors" were not traditionally viewed as corruption – and is a code of conduct substituting for the rule of law.

There are numerous examples to illustrate the intelligent development and use of *guānxì* by foreign companies ranging from General Motors to BP, Motorola, etc. One of the top oil companies employed the daughter of a very senior Party member to "open doors," this is considered a wise move; nobody in China will think anything different.

Guānxì and Networking

Much has been written about the similarity between *guānxì* and Western-style networking. We take the view that there are clear and subtle differences between the two.
Guānxì:

- Is focused and long-term.

- Involves relatively few contacts.

- Ties are always personal and trust based.

- Personal loyalty is more important than loyalty to an organization.

- Is motivated by both economic and social concerns.

- Has to be seen as part of a "holistic" ethos, embracing all the roles in Chinese life.

- Roles are characterized by an element of informality and flexibility

- Personal relationships can extend into organizational relation-ships, they are not perceived as separate entities.

On the other hand, networking:

- Is wide-ranging.

- Concerns acquaintanceship rather than friendship.

- Is a business relationship, with a group implication, not just a personal one.

- Makes a distinction between private and public spheres of contact.

- Is contract orientated.

- Is motivated primarily by economic concerns.

- Roles (in a networked relationship) are clearly defined and formal.

Managing "Corporate" *guānxì*

A persistent issue for foreign companies is the question of who owns the *guānxì* relationship. Many foreign companies employ a Chinese person to form the *guānxì* because he/she has the connections, speaks the language and intimately understands the culture. Because the person is employed by the company, Westerners assume their company owns the relationship. This is wrong. *Guānxì* transactions are always personally based. If employees leave the company they will take their *guānxì* with them, not hand it down to their replacements.

If this is not well managed, abuses can occur. In one example we know, the sales representatives of a beverage company obtained favorable credits for a distributor at the company's expense. This action not only enhanced the sales manager's connections, but was also a way of paying back favors from the past. It bought no benefit to the company at all, but was part of a larger process in which the company was merely a means to personal ends.

China commentator Wilfred Vanhonacker suggests the following processes to clarify this difficult grey area:

- Open the procurement process to competitive bidding. Currently, procurement is probably done via the *guānxì* network, which probably suits your procurement officer fine, but may not mean your company is getting the best deal.

- Develop a team-based approach. Many foreign companies are now moving to team-based selling and thus creating multiple points of contact, rather than the previous system whereby customer contact revolved around a particular individual. Note – this may not work well when dealing with government ministries, where the *guānxì* culture is still dominant.

- Develop loyalty-building activities in the company with your "frontline" Chinese employees. Examples might be allowing employees to bring their families to visit the company, or engaging with employees outside office hours in activities like visiting the fitness centre together. More radically, allow frontline staff to be managed by close friends of the management team or founder of the company. These activities have already been implemented by some companies in China.

One solution to the problem of staff abusing *guānxì* is to rotate sales and procurement people regularly. To Chinese, however, this is "cutting off your nose to spite your face." Connections are the essence of these functions. Find better ways of managing than this.

It is important for managers not to get paranoid about this. Salespeople in the West have been known to take clients with them when they leave! Sensible management procedures should ensure that the right balance is struck between personal and company interest.

Is *guānxì* Still Relevant in the 21st Century?

There is an argument in some circles that *guānxì* may be an outdated modus operandi to do business in China because

- China is rapidly developing cohesive regulatory and legal structures to facilitate business processes.

- Entry to WTO will facilitate Western-style business approaches.

- There is a growing, more professional, business cadre.

- More Chinese are being educated abroad or exposed to Western ways of doing business.

- Transaction costs are rising for "*guānxì*" relationships.

Given the above developments, *guānxì* could be perceived as an anachronism and a hindrance to proper, Western-style business. We would argue that in spite of these developments, *guānxì* will still have a critical role to play in Chinese businesses for a long time. It is part of the cultural fabric and one cannot simply eradicate a core feature like this.

Conclusion

Guānxì is essential to doing business in China. Without relationships, you are taking a leap in the dark, or as the Chinese say, "turning up at the temple door without a pig's head" (the traditional symbolic gift to heaven). The following guidelines may be helpful to avoid some of the pitfalls:

- Take time and effort to accumulate your network, and do not delegate this task.

- Always return favors – failure to do this results in "loss of face" all round and undoes any good work you have put into the relationship.

- *Guānxì* should be treated as a major part of your approach to your work life in China and not just an incidental accessory.

- Manage your *guānxì* like your bank account. After so many favors (credits), you will need to pay back (debits), even if it is not a convenient time to do so, in order to continue meet your obligations in the relationship and thus to retain face. The Chinese have turned this art into a carefully calculated science.

HARMONY (*HÉXIÉ*)

The Confucian concept of harmony has been discussed at some length in Chapter 2: the focus here is to give some practical examples to illustrate the working of this very important quality.

As mentioned earlier, the value of harmony embraces the concept of balance at both the individual and societal level.

On a personal level, the authors' Chinese parents instilled the notion that prosperity in life will only prevail once one has achieved a balance in one's life. That is, once you have achieved the balance in your life of being a good son or daughter, a good husband or good wife, a good father or mother and having a successful career, only then will you be harmonious in life. Until we have achieved all of these, we would not be in proper balance and therefore not in harmony, so we would not be truly happy or securely wealthy. As with many things, the Chinese invented work–life balance long before the West!

At the societal level, Chinese tradition focuses on harmony and the group. This can take many forms as the following examples illustrate:

- Showing off is considered poor behavior. An individual standing out from the crowd causes disharmony. This is the reasoning behind an old Chinese saying, often quoted with some disapproval in the West, as it runs so counter to prevailing notions of individual effort and attainment, that "the gun always fires at the first bird in the flock." But Western managers in China cannot ignore this aspect of the Chinese mindset.

    This has huge managerial implications for Western managers who want their Chinese employees to articulate their new ideas in a meeting or to come up with innovative suggestions or products. In the West, an individual who comes up with exciting and innovative suggestions is highly praised and feted. In China, being the first person to come up with innovative ideas in a group setting can have significant negative social implications. Furthermore, in China, imitation gives face.

    In China, the person who speaks up and produces original ideas can be seen as vulgar and foolish. As Lao Zi said, in the *Dao De Jing*: "He who knows, speaks not; he who speaks, knows not."

    These are very powerful drivers of group behavior in the workplace and a challenge to Western managers working in China.

- It is not uncommon in China for people to tell a little "white lie" with the simple intention of preserving harmony. This is in no way considered dishonorable – quite the opposite. For example, in China, it is customary not to tell very ill or even terminally ill patients how serious their illness is, in order to preserve harmony and peace of mind, and to prevent them being upset and losing their will to fight the disease. A good friend's father died without being told the type of disease he suffered from, this would be considered abhorrent in the West, but in China it is perceived as humane.

- Praising people is seen as a good thing, giving them face – as long as it is not done to excess. Excessive praise will embarrass a Chinese person – they fear it will endanger the social balance by giving the individual greater status than his or her peers.

- Discussing emotional or personal issues in public can damage group harmony. In the West this can act as a social bonding process by sharing problems collectively, but this can backfire in China.

- Because *guānxì* is about networks of people, an action that demeans one person can have a knock-on effect throughout an entire network. For example, if you become engaged in a conflict with someone, before you decide to take action such as suing him, you must make sure that you do not upset any intermediate relationship connected with this person and you. Everyone in the network is important: upsetting anyone in the network can lead to destabilizing the web of connections.

The above examples of, and about, face, *guānxì* and harmony should have demonstrated the close linking of these Confucian concepts, as illustrated in Figure 3.3. *Guānxì* is very much influenced by the Confucian qualities of "face" and "social harmony," all three are interrelated. If you conduct a sincere and honest relationship and respect a person's place in the hierarchy, this protects

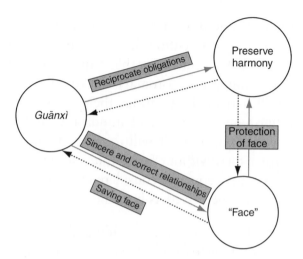

Figure 3.3 *Interlinking of Confucian concepts*

your position and that of others. In doing so, you will preserve social and individual harmony. If you reciprocate obligations and keep your promises, you preserve face.

THE FUTURE OF THESE TRADITIONS

China is changing fast and interacting with the West increasingly, and there are some who say China will inevitably find its culture being modified. We feel this is unlikely to be the case – more likely, the Chinese will become better at playing the Western game, but fundamentally our values and outlook are unlikely to change dramatically.

However some Chinese are asking themselves whether China can sustain its traditional cultural features in the face of globalization, which is driving China into many new markets and cultural influences. They point out that the "little emperor" generation (children of the one-child policy or Generation Y) appear to be rejecting many traditional notions and are said to be self-centered rather than family-centered and to have been spoilt by the "six parents" looking after them (the child's own parents, plus both sets of grandparents). China also has the problem of an aging population, and it is estimated that by 2025, there will be over

500 million people in China over the age of 50. The impact of both the one-child policy and aging population are forcing the Chinese to abandon deeply held values such as looking after their parents in old age. For example in Shanghai, some of the more affluent families are putting their parents into old people's homes – anathema to most Chinese.

But overall, there is still a strong belief in China that these changes will not be the norm. People you discuss this with often quote examples of overseas Chinese relations who cling to their traditional roots in a Western setting, often with even more tenacity than family members who are still in China.

When Deng Xiaoping was questioned whether his opening up to the West would have an effect on Chinese culture he simply commented that, "If you open a window, one or two flies might enter the room." Or, as Dr An Wang, the founder of the Wang Corporation in the USA in the 1950s, put it:

> A Chinese can never outgrow his roots. Ancient ideas such as Confucianism are as relevant today as they were 2,500 years ago. There is a practical genius to Chinese culture that allows it to assimilate new ideas without destroying old ones.

The three self-reinforcing core concepts of face, *guānxì* and harmony will continue to lie at the heart of Chinese society well into the twenty-first century. This new era will, in our view, be one of assimilation rather than one of cultural destruction.

CONCLUSION

We hope that in Chapters 1 and 2 we have given a sense of where Chinese leaders and employers derive their behavioral patterns and value perspectives. In this chapter we focused on what we considered are three key core cultural features and attributes that impact on the majority of transactions between Westerners and the Chinese.

The resulting differences are summed up in Table 3.1.

Table 3.1 *Chinese–Western cultural differences*

Chinese	Western
Paternalistic leadership style	Directive and open in communications
Group oriented	Individual oriented
Value harmony	Often have conflicting values
Avoid conflict	Confrontational
Authority and responsibility not specified	Authority and responsibility are specified
Group responsible for performance	Individual responsible for performance
Has long-term view	Short term view / need to show results
Feelings and relationships are paramount	Performance and "figures" paramount
Emphasize special nature of *guānxì*	Emphasize equality of individuals
Value age and hierarchy	Value personal achievement
Respect status and authority	Value freedom of expression

4
The Trust Challenge

From the discussion in the first three chapters of the book, we can identify cultural differences between Chinese and Western leaders and managers. Western managers come from a different perspective and value positions. Table 4.1 lists a number of the cultural differences as they apply *in the workplace*.

It shows that there are many challenges facing Western managers working in China – but they are not insurmountable. The table is a generic summary, and one would expect some variation depending on the type of organization being referred to, such as a SOE or MNC, the generation one is dealing with, and so on.

The cultural divide as shown in Table 4.1 poses many leadership challenges for Western managers operating in China, how they do apply Western management technology to a culture that is vastly different from theirs? It also raises the question of whether Western managers have the right competencies to be successful in China. What made Western managers successful in the West may not work well in China.

The focus of this chapter is to explore one element of this cultural divide where numerous misunderstandings have occurred consistently, that of truth and trust.

TRUTH AND TRUST

Let us take a simple example: the "face" concept. As we mentioned earlier, the Chinese will do almost anything to save face,

Table 4.1 *Chinese–Western cultural differences in the workplace*

Chinese	Western
Motivation – Social obligation, to serve society and be acknowledged	**Motivation** – Achievement, to prove one's worth
Accountability collective accountability	**Accountability** individual accountability
Authority – Obedience, prefer to follow leader follow the norms	**Authority** – Empowerment, creativity and initiative expected, seek self-development
Age and Hierarchy position & rank important, sex, marital status	**Equality** equal treatment of people, no age, sex or marital bias
Productivity – Encouraged, relationships vs. results	**Productivity** – Results oriented, performance appraisal process
Communications – Indirect and diffuse feedback is common	**Communications** – Direct and specific feedback

including a few white lies to preserve harmony. Or to put it another way, the Chinese prefer courtesy over truth in some situations, especially when face is at stake.

For example, it is quite common for Chinese employees leaving a company to tell their existing boss that they are leaving because a member of their family is ill or that their husband or wife has to move to another town, when in fact they are moving to employment with another company in the same city. This behavior is considered quite normal and acceptable. It is done because employees leaving want to show they are still very appreciative of what the company has done, and how highly they still think of the company. By telling what in the West would be seen as a devious, self-serving lie, they are actually acting to give face to the company.

It is unlikely that this will change dramatically in China in the coming years, even though the younger generation are more likely to adapt than the older Chinese workers.

The Western manager, for whom truthfulness is a core virtue, is faced with a dilemma. There are a number of possibilities here:

- Emphasize that the company culture requires correct information which is critical to a company's success. At the same time you could say that the Western manager too, will lose "face" if incorrect information is passed to headquarters. Many Chinese will understand the significance of this, though this, too, will be a hard battle.

- Make it clear to your team that your style of leadership is having the truth even if it is bad news, and that you prefer this type of communication. But you will need to continually reinforce this message: you will need bucket-loads of patience! It is also important to acknowledge to them that this type of "direct" communication is difficult for Chinese to handle and may cause them to lose face on a continual basis, which is also not good for team morale. Again, one needs to moderate this requirement until some level of trust is developed between you and your team. Remember that your team will give you respect because of your position, but will only begin to trust you once you behavior reflects your rhetoric. In the West, people may well start off trusting you till you prove otherwise: not so in China.

- At the same time, the Western manager also needs to learn to read the real meaning of the words that are said to them: learn to decode the "truth."

- Another approach is to personally select your own staff to work closely with you, as this engenders trust and loyalty. Or failing that, you could develop the trust of a few existing employees who understand Western ways and rely on them to give you the information as it is.

The above examples illustrate the cultural hurdles that many Western managers will need to overcome and how to decipher the

Chinese mindset to get a firm understanding of how to manage their Chinese workforce and become effective managers.

TRUST

When speaking to many Western managers or foreigners working with the Chinese, this is a major area of concern to them. In the earlier section about *guānxì*, we said that people only trust those with whom they have a very close relationship. This has implications for Chinese managers too, because at the corporate level, trust is a fundamental prerequisite: leader and subordinates need to trust each other.

In Western companies, there is at least an expectation that an implicit trust will exist when colleagues work together, because they share common goals and assumptions about where the company is going. In practice, of course, this trust is often abused or broken. However in China this expectation is even less likely to be realized.

One could say China is a low-trust society. This has always been the case – outside networks of *guānxì*, of course. The "Cultural Revolution" (1966–1976) no doubt exacerbated this even further. Relatives, friends, spouses and – most blasphemous of all to the Chinese – children were encouraged to report friends and family members to the authorities for noncompliance with certain rules and regulations, and for criticizing, or even appearing to criticize, the leadership. The generation after this appalling event became even less trusting and more suspicious than the previous generation.

The situation is even more complex in relations between Chinese and foreigners. In the nineteenth century China was invaded and conquered by Western nations. The ultimate expressions of this were perhaps the twin destructions of the Imperial Summer Palace in 1860 and 1900, both purely gestures of Western arrogance, to "show who was boss." The Chinese are a very proud race and such events are not taken lightly or forgotten quickly.

This makes the trust issue an even more tricky one for Westerners seeking to establish trust in China. Of course, as China increasingly comes into contact with foreigners, this wariness will be reduced over time. But in the meantime, there are some strategies that Western managers can perhaps use to reduce this suspicion and generate trust amongst the Chinese employees. According to Yue-er *et al.* (2008), the following steps could be taken to avoid the trust traps that one can fall into easily:

- Do not be too clannish or cliquish in the office setting; this sets off alarm bells for Chinese employees who perceive this as ganging up on the locals.

- In the canteen, make an effort to eat with the Chinese managers as much as possible in order to establish personal relationships with them. Of course, both sides, for cultural and linguistic reasons, tend to bunch together with those they feel comfortable with. So make a positive effort to overcome this.

- Sometimes, at the end of meetings, the expatriate head of the team requests the expatriate staff to stay behind for a few minutes and then the next day decisions are announced, which excluded Chinese counterparts. This will be perceived by local employees as a sign that they are not as valued and again deepens the mistrust in the organization

- A very common complaint made to me (but apparently rarely to non-Chinese consultants) is that many expatriate managers sent to China are very young and inexperienced but earn higher wages than experienced local staff. This raises the question of what is their added value. It may be the case that there is a justifiable rationale for this choice of expatriate, but it needs to be explained to the local staff.

- Develop local staff. Chinese staff often feel they do not receive the training that expatriates do.

- Do not tell Chinese staff: "This is how it is done back home, so this is how it is going to be done here." This smacks of ethnocentricity, arrogance and unwillingness to adapt to local conditions. Sadly, this is something we have come across again and again when working with multinational companies in China – usually when we have been asked in to find out why the Chinese staff are demotivated.

Building Trust in China

Apart from our own experiences, many people we work with in China tell us that Chinese people are very slow to trust each other, for reasons that we mentioned earlier on. Given the modernization drive now in train, and the need to respond quickly, people's attitudes are changing, albeit slowly. It is the foundation of leadership to gain trust. Building trust takes time: trust has to be earned, and trust in China is very difficult to gain. Unlike in the West, where trust is given first until proven otherwise, in China it's the opposite, like its legal system where "you are guilty till proven innocent." There are a number of strategies or approaches one can take to build this trust such as the following:

- In China, to gain trust you are judged by your deeds or behavior. So you need to deliver what you promised; only then will your staff begin the process of trusting you. Once trust is gained, however, your words will count for much. In this way, formal trust begins to take hold.

- To be a really effective leader, you also need to build personal trust with your team. You will need to invest time in this: what helps here is the sincere effort to socialize as much as you can outside office hours with members of your team. In China, socializing after work is a custom, one that is not common in the West. It is on these occasions that you share your personal data about your family, marriage, education, etc. which the Chinese love, and this breeds trust. We believe these are important steps to build trust. Only then can you begin to inculcate some of the key behaviors that you want your team to have; such as communicating upwards, giving you feedback, etc. This can only occur once team members feel sufficiently confident with you to express what they really think and feel.

- Making an attempt to understand Chinese history and culture will also endear you to your team and build trust to some extent; even better is attempting to learn the Chinese language. This will certainly help your relationship with staff. It is likely you will not be perceived as one of those "foreigners" coming to China to "rip us off," a common feeling about foreigners.

- Another useful technique to build trust is to have a participatory session with your team to develop a Team Charter or set of rules, which can be anything from "everyone's opinion counts," to "problems must be raised immediately," etc. Once these are established your team can then see if your actions, or anyone else's, are consistent with the Team Charter and thus establish further trust. But these rules must be developed jointly by, and communicated clearly to, all concerned parties.

- An important element for Western managers is to have feedback, which is a very Western management concept. Feedback is seen as critical to self-improvement and self-development. However, to get your Chinese subordinates to give you candid feedback will undoubtedly be difficult, though not impossible, because of the face issue, fear of authority, etc. It is safe to say that unless you have spent a long time in China, this task will be difficult to achieve naturally. One way round this is to be open and honest yourself, then your team will see this and reciprocate to some degree. You will need to take a chance and start trusting your team with small risks and they will get the message. Hopefully your team will respond appropriately to your gestures and open up.

TRUST AT THE NATIONAL LEVEL

Trust is also an issue at the national level. It is quite common to hear in the West, "You can't trust the Chinese. They'll steal intellectual property, welsh on negotiated deals and many of them are corrupt." The reality is that business in China operates by different rules to those in the West. The key to developing one's judgment in China is to understand the rules, and thus learn the difference between someone who is fundamentally honest but playing by different rules from you, and someone who is an out-and-out crook, with whom local people would have no truck.

There will, of course, be crooks, for obvious reasons. One is simply numbers: there are a lot of Chinese and a proportion will be "rotten apples." China is also emerging from the shadows of socialism, where commercial activities were all frowned upon: business ethics are a new topic for many people. Add the fact that there is little transparency or regulatory enforcement – and also the traditional Chinese determination to get rich – and you cannot expect perfection! Remember that the problem is not exclusive to China: look at the former Eastern European and Russian economies. Of course, we do not condone such people, but there are also plenty of honest (by local standards) businesspeople out there.

Do not fall into the trap that we have seen some foreigners fall into, of using ethical high-mindedness as a cover-up for cultural misunderstandings. "Those devious ***s cheated us" may feel better than "We failed because we didn't understand the culture," but it doesn't lead to learning or to good management.

The Great IPR Swindle

Let us look more closely at one area that concerns Western companies in China, that of Intellectual Property Rights (IPR). It is no secret that China is currently the world's largest producer of counterfeit products, infringing patents, copyright and trademarks to produce all sorts of things from designer clothes to computer software. The Chinese government's own Development Research Council estimates that counterfeiting in China is a $30 billion industry. From a Western perspective, such actions cannot be condoned. However, the phenomenon needs to be examined more closely.

The Software Publishers' Association carried out surveys in different countries asking whether people thought it right to use software without paying for it. The majority of respondents in Western countries agreed that this was wrong (although there is plenty of software sharing in the West: what people say and what they do are often not the same thing). In countries with strong Confucian traditions the practice was seen as less unethical. Confucian culture puts stress on individuals sharing what they create with the group and society. Infringements of IPR are not seen as theft in the way that stealing someone's purse would be.

A traditional story tells of a very poor boy in imperial times – when there was no state education and all lessons had to be paid for – who had to leave school because his parents ran out of money. This boy secretly went to the school and hid himself under the windowsill to listen to the teachers. Eventually he passed the imperial examination with flying colors and achieved official rank in the government. The boy has always been portrayed as heroic, overcoming barriers to study. Confucius claimed in the *Analects* that "in education, there is no discrimination" which means everyone is entitled to be educated including those who can afford it and those who cannot. Therefore people pursing education by any means are admired in China.

This propensity to break "rules" is partly conditioned by Confucian philosophy, which values the "rule of man" over the "rule of law." Further, China has also had 4,000 years of authoritarian rule. In this time, the Chinese had laws imposed on them by different emperors, some benevolent and others brutal. This has given rise to a mentality whereby Chinese people uphold the rules publicly but flout them when they have to (and when they believe they can get away with it). It is a survival strategy. Hence there is a tendency not to feel guilty about ignoring or circumventing the system. Much Chinese behavior can be described as driven by expediency, by the need to get by in an often harsh world.

Finally, many Chinese see the Western "fuss" about IPR as an attempt by developed countries to monopolize technically advanced products.

Some commentators do not accept the argument that China's culture creates a different attitude to IPR than is found elsewhere. It is a matter of political will, not culture, they say. This attitude displays their ignorance and arrogance. IPR violations occur in the first place because of cultural attitudes formed from thousands of years of subverting the system in China.

At the same time, IP theft is not just a Chinese but a global problem. It is not unknown in the West! China is the top source of counterfeit electronic components; approximately 10 percent to 40 percent of electronics goods in China today are believed to be fake. The estimated figure for the Middle East is 20 percent to 40 percent, and for Eastern Europe it is around 10 percent to 40 percent. Asian countries such as Korea, Vietnam, and India; and some South American countries significantly contribute to the overall IPR violations. So counterfeiting is truly a global problem. Mentioning this does not in any way condone China's role in this matter; but it does raise questions about the kind of countermeasures to take. Effective policing should be global and not China-centric only, as this may be ineffective in countering IPR violations.

The problem is no longer so much about the existence of laws or a general will to enforce them. The sheer size of China complicates the implementation of all legislation. The topic is a relatively new one, and many people are still unaware of it.

The Chinese problem is one of enforcement, which is not yet up to international standards, however, IP protection is improving in China. China is eager to abide by WTO conventions, and is developing laws on IPR. And as Chinese technology companies become more innovative, pressure for IPR protection are rising in China. China wants to protect its own domestic technology companies. In late 2010, Chinese police arrested over 1,700 suspects and uncovered 676 cases of IPR infringement worth a total of over $125 million The victims of violation of IPRs included Chinese and foreign companies, such as China's "national liquor" producer Moutai, computer manufacturer Lenovo, Louis Vuitton and Nike.

What Can Foreign Companies Do About IPR Violations In China?

Things are getting better. IPR consciousness is rising in China, due in part to court cases, access to the Internet and the Chinese media's coverage of violations. China has an obligation as a signatory of TRIPs (Agreement on Trade-related Aspects of Intellectual Property Rights) to maintain an effective regime for the protection of IPRs. In 2010, over 1,057 foreign-related IPR infringement cases were handled by Chinese courts, some of the big names were involved such as Sony, BMW, Pfizer, HP and Microsoft.

Between 2006 and November 2010 about 55.2 percent of the 2,691 foreign-related IPR cases were given support or partial support. The message is not to be apathetic to China's IPR system and to take stringent action in cases of violation, following the examples of these companies mentioned above. The Chinese government recently launched a national campaign to crack down on violations of intellectual property rights. The focus of the Campaign lasted the six months from October 2010 to March 2011 and was very comprehensive in scope. This campaign was also driven by China's own national economic interests because at the 5th Plenary session of the 17th National Congress of the Communist party of China (CPC), it was made clear that the 12th Five-Year Program will focus on scientific development and accelerating the transformation of the economic development pattern. The tools for transforming the economic development landscape will be scientific and technological, which are easy prey to IPR violations. So we believe this a campaign that will strengthen foreign investors' confidence in China's efforts to improve its IPR environment. We have observed a gradual crackdown on IPR violations at street level. A few years ago one would constantly be approached in the street, restaurants and bars by hawkers peddling counterfeit CDs and DVDs. In 2011 this activity has been reduced substantially. Yes, it still happens, but not on the scale of the previous years. How much this represents the true scale of crackdown overall is debatable, but, nevertheless, something is stirring.

5
Business Leadership in Modern China

In China, there are three main types of commercial organization: the State Owned Enterprise (SOE), the Multinational Company (MNC) and the Chinese Private Company (CPC). SOEs and CPCs have existed for 30 years; MNCs became part of the mix 10 years later, in the early 1990s. These three types are very different in their organizational structure and culture, and thus in the kind of leadership exercised within them.

An SOE is government-run. Its primary purpose is to pursue the interests of the state: financial profit comes second. Social stability and harmony is paramount. It is highly centralized, hierarchical and formal. People working in an SOE look not just for a career in business but one in government. Confucian culture and leadership based on Humane Theory are predominant in this sector.

MNCs are disliked: they are seen as the vassal of foreign empire. Naturally, profit maximizing is their main pursuit. These organizations are decentralized, with flat structure and systematic operation processes; people within them are driven by personal development, financial reward and promotion. MNCs provide a relatively democratic environment with a Western leadership style – largely done by expatriates.

A CPC is mainly a family-run business. It is highly centralized, autocratic and paternalistic. As the owner is the only one to determine structure, process and culture, this sector is like an experimental field: you may see all types of culture and leadership. Mohism and Altruistic leadership prevail to some extent.

For many Chinese in search of a career, an SOE is the first option because of job security, political options, and social status as a "Red Hat," linked to government which is still the most powerful agent in the Chinese business world. Furthermore, the Confucian maxim "To be a state official is the ultimate individual pursuit" is still very influential. An MNC is the second most popular option, especially for people who wish to be professional managers and to get good pay. The "Foreign Comprador" may not be liked but is grudgingly respected.

A CPC is the least popular choice, except for career transit or short-term high pay. The stereotype of "Peasant Entrepreneurs" still prevails.

LEADERSHIP CHALLENGES AT SOEs

There are approximately 150,000 SOEs, of which about 155 are large ones. These are still under the direct management of a government body, SASAC (State Assets Supervision and Administration Committee). This retains tight control, despite the movement to "separate government functions from enterprise management" that has been under way since 1978 and pushed hard since 2001.

In 2010, the biggest SOEs, Sinopec (China Petroleum Corporation) and State Grid, were ranked No.7 and 8 in the Fortune Top Global 500. For both, the top management team – Chairman, CEO and senior VPs – is actually appointed by the Ministry of Organization of the Central Committee of the Party and by SASAC. All these leaders have positions both in their companies and the national government; for example, the Chairman of Sinopec has a ministerial position.

Most of these leaders have a background of higher education in science, alongside experience in government. Few of them are accomplished in Western management (and actually few of them know much about Chinese traditional philosophies – which does not, of course, mean that they are not influenced by these!).

Most of them "lead" their organization in the context of a vision and strategy set by government: to be a business leader in this sector is to be a politician rather than an entrepreneur.

For example, in the 2009 oil crisis, the price of crude oil reached a peak of $140 per barrel but the Chinese government kept the price of petrol unchanged at $1.5 per gallon in order to stabilize the market and society. Just one of Sinopec's subsidiaries lost $38 million per month at this time. The job of this subsidiary's CEO was to keep his team's morale up, as well as his own, while adapting to this aspect of China's "planned market economy."

As befits a former government entity, SOE culture is about strong social cohesion and collective thinking. Individual proactiveness and initiative-taking do not flourish. Perpetual relocation of senior management is a fact of life in an SOE and leads to short-term oriented organizational development.

The staff turnover at SOEs is relatively low; most middle management and above have worked for the organization since they graduated. The "official status" and "iron rice bowl" heritage is the main part of their psychological contract. ("Iron rice bowl" occupations are seen as offering guaranteed job security, as well as steady income and benefits.) Usually, management at SOEs like to be addressed by their political title rather than their business title – as "Deputy General Wang" instead of "Manager Wang."

In comparison with the other two types of organization, the SOE is the most formal in terms of organizational structure, hierarchy and degree of power-distance. Despite this, managers often get things done informally through their influence rather than authority.

Unlike the case in other Chinese companies, Human Resources (HR) plays a key role in SOEs. The HR function called "Cadre Administration" has the job of assessing and supervising middle management and above. It is they who make the major decisions on staff recruitment and promotion, not line managers or general managers of business units, even though these people know the individuals involved much better. If HR says "No," the chance of "Yes" is tiny.

The main recruitment drive by SOEs is among new graduates. They are by and large not interested in recruiting talents from other companies, especially from MNCs and CPCs. The result is an "inbred" culture.

SOE employees cannot be sacked unless they make fatal mistakes such as criminal infringements. It is not a joke that an SOE CEO would find it difficult to sack a gate-keeper.

Salaries are fixed according to government guidelines. The average income of middle management and above is much lower than in MNCs and CPCs, and the salary gap within levels of the organization is small. For example, in 2009 the annual salary of the CEO of one of the large listed SOEs was only $40,000. Promotion is hard to secure, as there is a strict quota for each department. Some people cite the above as justification for their "grey incomes," alongside the high level of inflation in major Chinese cities.

The biggest challenge for SOE managers is to motivate and retain talented people. Creating high—performance teams is particularly difficult. Managers also have to accept responsibility for all team members – including those who are not qualified but cannot be dismissed.

There are three layers in large SOEs.

- *Top management,* called "Party Committee Members," consists of Chairman, CEO, and Senior VPs. These people normally have a solid background in both government and enterprise. Most of them don't have management education or training. They focus on politics and strategy in line with the government. Their leadership styles vary but they are often energetic, eloquent, charismatic and assertive.

- *Upper-middle management,* called "Director-General Cadre," includes heads of business units, presidents and vice presidents of manufacturing or of subsidiaries. These people, mostly experts on various technical fields, manage daily business and most employees: they are the backbone of SOEs. Since early 2000, large SOEs have sent upper-middle managers to overseas universities for management/leadership training. Although they learn Western management concepts there, most of them find these difficult to apply when they get back, due to the SOE culture and structure.

- *Middle management*, called "Section Chief Cadre," are departmental managers focusing on daily tasks. Some of them have MBA or management education background, but given the SOE culture there is not much flexibility for them to exercise the Western approach.

Most SOE leaders exercise their leadership in the following ways:

- Their key skill is influencing.

- They are prudent, conservative, on any initiatives.

- They take a long time to make decisions. Consensus has to be reached with all parties in order to avoid unpredicted and unnecessary conflicts.

- They are happy to change plans to comply with superiors.

- They are modest and polite towards to foreign people, who are seen as guests.

- They are controlling: they keep an eye on all processes and need frequent feedback on each step.

- They motivate people through personal relationship and charisma.

- They act as role models for hard work and willingness to compromise personal life. "Working on Saturday is guaranteed, and taking a day off on Sunday is not guaranteed" is the slogan.

- Their attitude to superiors is "Ready within call."

- They are relationship-oriented and respect authority.

- They have great political astuteness. "Political correctness" is superior to pure business decisions.

- Their dress is the same as normal staff, in order to be accessible. It is common practice that GMs of manufacture wear worker's uniform at work, so do some Chinese GMs working for Joint Ventures.

Irrespective of their "Red Hat" privilege, SOE leaders need high EQ to survive and achieve their goals. There is not huge scope for imaginative, big-picture leadership: the government is still at the wheel.

Fu Chengyu, one of the star leaders at an SOE, may offer a glimpse of Chinese leaders in this sector.

Fu was born in 1951 into a poor family in northern China; he worked for CNOOC (China National Offshore Oil Corporation) from 1982, when it was established in response to the policy of separating government functions from enterprise management. He graduated as a geology major from a local college, and he was one of a few SOE leaders to get a foreign degree, a n MSc in Petroleum Engineering from Southern California University.

Fu was appointed on April 8 2011 as the Chairman of Sinopec (considered the giant of SOEs). Before this appointment, he had been the CEO of CNOOC from 2003, and he is also a Member of the Central Committee of Discipline Inspection of the CPC (Communist Party of China).

Compared to the majority of SOE leaders, Fu is seen as "Westernized," because he has an American university qualification, he speaks English fluently and he has worked with foreign partners such as Amoco, Chevron, Texaco, CnoocPhilips, and Shell, for more than two decades. He chaired the strong, eight-person board, including four foreigners as nonexecutive directors. Yet he was in charge of the third-largest oil company in China, which is ranked 20 in the Fortune Top 500 in 2010. Amongst large SOEs, CNOOC is considered the most market-driven global-standard organization, and now he is at the wheel.

Fu is renowned for his audacity in leading China's biggest overseas M&A initiative of $18.5 billion, seeking to acquire Unocal, the ninth-largest oil company in the USA, in 2005. Although CNOOC was Unocal's first choice as a merger partner, this marriage was eventually to founder because of the opposition from Washington, as "Some beltway politicians would paint CNOOC, which is 70 percent state-owned, as an arm of a Communist government out to strip the U.S. of vital energy supplies." ("Uncharted Waters," Bill Powell, *Time*, July11, 2005.)

The bid for Unocal is by far the most audacious move which a Chinese SOE has made. Fu, the tall, dark, fit and energetic SOE leader, was really ambitious and believed that he could make it happen, given his experience and understanding of Western culture and business.

Fu may not be a sophisticated politician in the global arena, and he could not convince the US government of his argument of "We are a transparent company, and this is a good deal for Unocal's shareholders and its employees." Even sources close to CNOOC's board told *Time* that "Fu, not some shadowy string-pulling figure in Beijing, has been the driving force behind the bid." He is a reputable business leader who has been granted several awards in China, and is seen as a vanguard to lead SOEs to compete in the world market.

To many SOE leaders who are executing a "go out" strategy set by the Chinese government, the resistance Fu encountered illustrates probably the biggest challenge to their ambitions in the international market. Fu was educated in the US and "the most Westernized Chinese business leader": his complex feelings are probably revealed in his speech at Qinghua University, "Anyone, even though he is extremely capable, would not be able to perform without the backing of his own country."

The fundamental leadership skill for SOE leaders is balancing politics and business initiatives. Failure to do so, no matter how capable you are, can lead to charges of "corruption" or "staying in the wrong queue," which means following the wrong people. The consequences of these failures can be grave: recently a former CEO of a large SOE was arrested at a meeting, and another one was expelled from his office.

The challenges of the SOE CEO's role are well summed up by Wei Jiafu, CEO of COSCO (China Ocean Shipping Corporation): "A SOE leader needs to be five people in one: a politician, a philosopher, an artist, a diplomat and a doer."

LEADERSHIP CHALLENGES AT MNCs

Working at MNCs was a desirable career path in China until recently, when SOEs and CPCs increased their employee welfare to attract talent at the same time as MNCs began cost cutting as the global financial crisis bit.

Apart from decent pay and individual recognition, people have a sense of honor working at MNCs due to their advanced management techniques, profound global industry know-how and, in the background, the cachet of Western civilization.

Most employees focus on personal development and work towards goals that result quickly in promotion and pay rises. Employees can openly pursue their individual ambitions, and are delegated to make their own decisions due to the flat structure. They tend to be concerned more about their personal achievement than the rise or decline of the organization.

Most MNCs implement their "global practice" in China by adjusting to local requirements, so call their approach "glocal." Or so they say; in practice, only a few Chinese people have been promoted to senior positions in MNCs. The sense of belong is still relatively weak: Chinese executives rather see themselves "Professional Managers" than "Leaders,' whose key role is to implement and comply with the vision and strategy made by foreign leaders sitting in the overseas headquarters.

The view of Chinese employees is that an MNC is a training school for management skills and professionalism, and it is normal to jump from one MNC to another for better salary and position.

There is a sense that the Chinese always have this haunting feeling that they "depend on someone for a living" especially with respect to foreigners. This sometimes results in the Chinese over-reacting to foreigners in debates and discussions. These feelings sow the seeds for potential conflict between Chinese managers and their foreign partners in the workplace. Furthermore, the situation is not helped sometimes by the actions of expatriates, who act in a way considered insensitive by the Chinese and this exacerbates an already tense situation. It is not unusual for some foreign CEOs to be asked to leave their position in China because of inappropriate actions such as a speech which is not culturally sensitive. Sometimes, expatriate managers are asked to leave their positions because of a mismatch between them and their Chinese local team.

Although an MNC has many advantages for the talented Chinese manager compared to SOEs and CPCs, there is rarely a chance for a Chinese to get a senior management position at corporate level: the ceiling a Chinese can reach is the country head, "CEO for China," which is upper-middle management rather than the very top.

In a few cases local Chinese mangers have been promoted to top levels at reputed MNCs such as Microsoft, Cisco and GE Medical, but most of them left within five years. The cultural mismatch was too great for the Chinese managers in these companies. A few stars among them were recruited as a CEO at CPCs, but most of them ended up hunting new MNC employers.

Chinese managers working for MNCs normally are of one of two types.

The first type have experiences of both SOE and MNC culture, and they tend to be more adaptable and use various leadership styles depending on the situation. They can be very "Chinese" or very "Westernized," depending on what the circumstances require. Their attitude is "When in Rome, do as the Romans do."

Foreign bosses often accuse Chinese managers of suddenly becoming "very Chinese" when they are promoted to lead business units. What has happened is that these managers have finally been put in a position where they can – and have to – return to their roots. They believe, largely correctly, that as a Chinese, you can only mange your countrymen effectively in a Chinese way, otherwise you will be perceived as a "flunky of foreigners" or a "fake foreign devil" by them. Problems occur when the "nationalism nerve" is pressed by foreign managers, usually unintentionally, and Chinese managers are expected (by their Chinese subordinates) to take the Chinese side even if the foreign manager was right.

Tang Jun is a public figure, known as "Emperor of Employees." He is the role model for Chinese employees working for an MNC, and has won several business awards as a professional manager.

Tang was born in the 1960s. He was educated in China, Japan and the USA, and he returned to China in the early 1990s. As a "Sea Turtle," he successfully landed at Microsoft in 1994. Tang had been continuously promoted because of his outstanding achievement, especially under his leadership: Microsoft China was the only Microsoft branch whose sales continuously increased for six months in 2003. Tang reached the ceiling as a Chinese in 2002 as the CEO for China; two years later, he retired with the title of "Honorary Life CEO of Microsoft China."

As usual, Tang was not able to grow further in the "colony." He joined a CPC – SNDR – as its CEO. He did well given the "cultural shock" of moving from MNC to CPC and stayed for four years. Since then, he has remained in the CPC field and has been the CEO of New Huadu Industrial Group since 2008.

Tang tried running his own business for a short time in his early days, but since then his career has been as a professional manager. He believes that personality determines one's destiny, and in addition, that diligence, passion, opportunity and wisdom will lead to success as a professional manager.

Tang could thrive in different business cultures, thanks to his ability to balance flexibility and professionalism. When he worked for Microsoft he hardly worked more than 8 hours a day, yet he stayed in the office for 12 hours a day for two years when he worked for SNDR, to earn the recognition of his subordinates.

Tang's boss at SNDR asked him to recruit several people from Microsoft; he kept his professionalism as well as his boss's face by convincing his boss that SNDR had enough talents who just needed to be recognized and developed, and there was no need to get anyone from outside. Tang actually became a controversial public figure, he published several books on how to manage business, and he was also questioned about the authenticity of his PhD degree. Tang even said, "The shortcut to promotion is to behave, achieve and show."

The second type is those who only have working experience at MNCs. After graduating, locally or overseas, they grew up in the MNC "colony" and have been developed as Western leaders. They are more "Westernized" than the first echelon. They tend to be more open and direct. Sometimes they find it easier to work with foreign colleagues than Chinese ones.

As a result it is a huge challenge for them to lead Chinese blue-collar workers, as they are expected to behave in a Chinese way but have never encountered the Chinese way of leading. Most of these people will stay at MNCs for rest of their career, as they would suffer severe cultural shock at CPCs or SOEs. There have been several cases recently where Chinese managers of this type job-hopped to CPCs as senior management, and had to return to MNCs only after few months.

Many expatriates working in MNCs are puzzled that their Chinese colleagues are nice but somehow distant or resistant even if they (the expatriates) were not arrogant, abusive or insensitive. Some Chinese employees have conflicting feelings: they are proud of working for a globally recognized company, but at the same time they have a feeling of being a "second class citizen" within that company.

The expatriate must understand that they do not belong to the Chinese community; as an outsider, they are either a representative of the "landlord," there to supervise "Chinese workers," or a temporary guest in China Town. Either way, the expat can be treated very nicely if they are a friendly representative of the landlord or sensible guest – but if the expat shows off "privilege," they can easily become a "public enemy."

Chinese rules of who's inside and who's outside are powerful and deeply ingrained. Chinese have been brought up with maxims such as "be severe with family members and lenient towards guests," "be united towards outsiders," and "discriminate between insiders and outsiders."

These conventions have both positive and negative implications. They also explain why some Chinese managers can get more resistance than foreign managers from their Chinese teams.

LEADERSHIP CHALLENGES AT CPCs

The CPC sector is now tantamount to a new "Warring States" situation, i.e. similar to the "Wild West" in the USA in the early 20th century, with only the vaguest rules and regulations. There are approximately 3 million CPCs out there. Apart from the leading brands such as Lenovo, Haier and TCL, most of them are still in the primitive stage in terms of organizational structure, management process and leadership. The average life cycle of CPCs is three years. And in Zhong Guan Cui, "The Silicon Valley of China," out of 5,000 CPCs only 430 have survived for five years. One of the successful entrepreneurs of a CPC said "If I were in a real market economy country, I would not have chance of succeeding," meaning that the CPC sector is still in the throes of developing in an immature market, and therefore he was able to exploit opportunities in an unregulated sector.

Most CPCs are family businesses; regardless of their capabilities, family members occupy all important positions. Often, the husband is Chairman and CEO, the wife or daughter is CFO, the brother or son is COO. They manage their own functions in their own ways, a narrow-minded paternalistic culture dominates the company, and the chairman ends up being a dictator with "One voice." And finally his/her entrepreneurial spirit, as well as the company, either sinks in a marsh of "yes men" or is ripped apart by factionalism.

Most of these entrepreneurs rise from obscurity. In the early 1980s, when Deng encouraged all people to do business, the first cohort to respond was composed of jobless, farmers, people dismissed from SOEs, uneducated, and released criminals. In the late 1990s, the second cohort appeared, including retired government officials, military officers and people who had resigned from SOEs.

It is axiomatic that some of them made their first bucket of gold no matter whether they were "white cats" or "black cats." Their key success factor was their audacity: they did not have any benchmarks to follow and made it with their own judgments and intuitions. This could backfire; lacking legal knowledge, it took some of them a couple of years to turn from a star entrepreneur to a prisoner. An irrational decision-making mindset is the inveterate habit of most CPC managers; as they say, "Pat the forehead to make the decision, pat the chest to guarantee the implementation, and finally pat the bottom to leave the job."

Three decades later, those entrepreneurs that survived became heroes in this business greenwood. Now, when they enter a stage of more formal, corporate growth, they still exercise their leadership in the way they used to as "Greenwood Heroes," driven by personal feelings and relationships and neglecting fairness, rules and principles. Although they are admired by their followers for their assertiveness, perseverance, courage, brotherliness, eloquence and charisma, they tend to be autocratic, irrational, unserious, subjective, changeable, nontransparent and unprincipled.

To ensure a healthy transition to a more formal corporate entity, some CPCs recruit a professional manager from an MNC as a CEO to build systematic management and operational structures. However, these arrangements tend not to last. As the former CEO

Niu Gensheng is a star entrepreneur in China. He was an orphan, adopted by a herdsman in inner-Mongolia in late 1950s. He then became a dairyman in the late 1970s. He was the Vice President of Yili Dairy Corporation, one of five largest dairy companies in China, from 1983 to 1998. He was a charismatic leader and in charge of a unit generating 80 percent of total revenue. Niu was dismissed by the President, who felt threatened by Niu's power and cried out in a board meeting, "Yili, either take him and expel me, or vice versa."

In 1999, Niu established his own company, Mengniu Dairy, with approximately 120,000 shares from Yili, where his hundred followers also came from. Since then, Mengniu has grown rapidly: within four years Mengniu became no.1 in the dairy market, and was recognized as a "miracle" of Chinese industry. In 2002, Mengniu was nominated the "fastest growing enterprise" having grown its revenues from $5 million to $1 billion within 24 months. In 2003, it became the first mainland company listed in Hong Kong.

In 2004, Niu donated all of his shares to establish the "Old Niu (old cow) Foundation." (The Chinese surname of Niu is also the name for a cow.) He resigned respectively from his position as CEO in 2006, and Chairman in 2009. Interestingly, the CEO of COFCO (a SOE) took over the position of Chairman.

Niu is a "Greenwood Hero" who rose up in revolt against his old employer and built up his own empire. He still has the habits of a dairyman, wearing a $3 tie. He believes that the IQ leads to short-term success and MQ (Moral intelligence) leads to lasting success. He likes to read the *Dao De Jing* of Lao Zi, which may have influenced him in his decision to retire from his crown; it was perhaps a wise decision in this time of "unprotected Warring States."

of a large CPC said, "In this sector, you can't trust the Chairman, because he/she is not the Chairman but the CEO with the title of Chairman. The CEO this person has recruited is actually the COO or the Chairman's assistant."

Some CPC leaders have tried to equip themselves with modern management skills by enrolling in MBA classes. However, apart from networking, how much they benefit from the academic environment remains an open question.

The CPC sector plays key role in the fast-growing Chinese market. It accounts for 92 percent of total business organizations in the country, 61 percent of GDP and provides 100 million employment opportunities. However, its leadership style can be classified as 95 percent "Greenwood Hero," 4 percent Taylorism, and 1 percent Humane leadership. A few CPC bosses have made the leap to being real model corporate leaders, Zhang Ruimin of Haier and Liu Chuanzhi of Lenovo for example. For the rest, there is still a long way to go for them to possess the leadership skills compatible with the growth of their organizations.

Table 5.1 shows the management background at each type of organization.

THE JOB MARKET

On the supply side, there are enormous human resources available in China, in 2010, the number of new graduates was about 6.3 million, and it appears that the talent pool is huge.

But the number of jobless and the demand for talent is equally high. The composition of current human resources is a diamond shape; the two sharp ends, where demand outstrips supply, are qualified management and blue-collar workers. Due to the shortage, the MNC finds it difficult to keep a mediocre accounting manager even though they pay much higher than the international standard, and sometimes, the hotel General Manger has to go to a job fair to try to recruit cleaners.

The huge middle part of diamond is taken up by degree holders without much work experience, who are neither able to manage nor willing to take "unworthy" blue-collar jobs. Due to the revival of Confucianism, the mindset of "value education above all else" is predominant in society. Unfortunately, the "spoon-feeding" methods of Chinese education are not a cradle of business leaders.

Table 5.1 *Management backgrounds, by organization type*

Position	SOE	MNC	CPC
Senior management	Government official; "Red Hat Merchant"; Chinese education; working for government and SOEs	Expatriate; Western education	Chinese entrepreneur - Overseas returnees "sea turtle"; working experience of MNC, Chinese and western education - Scholar "Confucian merchant"; working experience of government and SOEs; Chinese education - Farmer "Peasantry entrepreneur"; no other working experience, under-educated - Others
Upper-middle management	Local Chinese; expert, major in engineering or science; Chinese education; working for SOE only	Expatriate, overseas returnee, local Chinese; working experience including MNCs and SOEs; Chinese and Western education	Local Chinese, working experience including MNCs and CPCs; Chinese and Western education; special relationship with businesses owners
Middle management	Local Chinese; Chinese education; working for SOE only	Expatriate, overseas returnee, local Chinese; working experience including MNCs and SOEs; Chinese and Western education	Local Chinese, working experience of CPCs; Chinese education

CONCLUSION

In this overheated market, the SOEs are in the process of moving out from the "protection umbrella" of government under pressure from the WTO agreement. MNCs are losing some of the benefits of the "most-favored-clause," whereby they previously had tax holidays, preferential treatment from the government departments, etc. Now, they are claiming that the environment for foreign investment has "deteriorated." CPCs are the rising stars though struggling with growing pains.

Will the current cohort of Chinese business leaders be able to lead their organizations to cope with the pace of economic growth? There are 43 Chinese mainland organizations listed in the Fortune Top 500 in 2010, including one CPC (Ping An Insurance). If there were no support or protection from government, would the 42 SOEs remain the same place? Compared to MNCs, both SOEs and CPCs are still in their adolescence in terms of global experience and industrial know-how; both need new-generation leaders who have both solid Chinese background and Western experience, but their current systems and cultures impede the influx of talents from MNCs.

FEMALE LEADERSHIP

Not much has been written about female leadership in China in this book. Although this topic could justify a book in its own right, we felt that a cursory investigation of this topic would be a useful introduction to a potentially fascinating area for the future. We would like to give a very brief background to the history of the role of Chinese women in China; and then explore some examples of female leaders in modern China.

Historical Background

Two men in Chinese history have determined the destiny of Chinese women. Confucius might not have discriminated against women, but, at the least, he seems to have been allergic to them. In his time, a man could have a wife and countless concubines,

Confucius had only one and even made her redundant because she was domestically incompetent.

His infamous quotation "small men and women are difficult to deal with" had the effect of making Chinese women inferior for thousands of years. Phrases such as "ignorance is the virtue of a woman" and "beauty is dangerous" unfortunately shackled Chinese women for centuries.

Mao Zedong was the second man who changed the fate of Chinese women; he liberated them and offered equal opportunity for education and jobs. He praised women as "holding half of the sky." Ironically, his two wives sacrificed themselves for his revolution, and his last infamous wife sacrificed the country.

In feudal times, Chinese women were objects kept at home, their pursuit was to make themselves desirable in order to please men. "A woman is to be dressed up to impress a man" was their daily life and in return, they were loved, protected and defended. Conditioned for thousands of years, most Chinese women have a strong gender-consciousness, and believe that the world is dominated by men. They do not believe in equality: they really believe that when compared to men, they are the weaker sex, and not surprisingly, some of them play their female side or victim role to survive or attain achievement in society.

In Mao's time, it was the opposite situation. Chinese women were educated to have less gender-consciousness, equality was extended even to the physical level of work – women were encouraged to work and dress like men, and many Chinese women were engaged in heavy manual work such as steel-making and road-work. Unfortunately, this made them suffer physically for the rest of their lives because of their ignorance of bio-physical knowledge. "Iron-girl" or "tomboy" was the role model for women at that time. Femininity was seen as the province of either the "bourgeoisie" or a "prostitute." However, even during this period, Chinese women did not believe that they were equally as good as men, they just restrained their feminine side and behaved like a man.

Given the historical background, in China, we do not have real feminism by Western definitions or standards. There is no neutral concept for both men and women even in the workplace. Chinese men respect a female colleague as a woman rather than as a person; they might praise her beauty rather than her intelligence. It would be safe to say that in China, in general, for many men, a beautiful woman is admirable, but an intelligent woman is threatening.

Most Chinese women would prefer that men saw them first as a woman, then as a friend or colleague. Some of them would even react to a man's behavior as a female first. For instance, if a man kissed his female colleague's cheek, she may either think he is taking advantage of her or he loves her. It took quite a long time for some Chinese women to realize that their foreign male colleagues doing this was just another form of a greeting like a handshake.

In Chinese history, there have been two powerful female rulers. Wu Zetian (624–705 AD) of the Tang Dynasty was the only legitimate female emperor and contributed to the glory of that dynasty, which is recognized as the heyday of feudal China. The second was the infamous Cixi who was the "power behind the throne," and lost the opium war to a foreign woman (Queen Victoria). Both Wu Zetian and Cixi lived in the shadow of men as the emperors' concubines and played their female side to reach the peak.

Chinese women have been shackled both spiritually (as they were not allowed to be educated) and physically (bound feet) for thousands of years; they have now developed perseverance, resilience and tenacity but they are emotionally dependent and vulnerable-looking though they have strong hearts.

From what has been briefly discussed, one can appreciate how challenging it is to be a woman leader in China, especially at the SOE and CPC organizations. There are few female leaders at ministerial level in government and at senior management level in the SOE; and those who are leaders in these organizations are not married nor have children. They come across as tough and unfeminine, which may be why they are successful in the Chinese culture. On the other hand, some women have to play their female side to ascend to the hierarchy of their organizations. The professional women in the West is likely to find it extremely

Xie Qihua was the Chairwoman and CEO for 12 years of Bao Steel, one of the large SOEs, ranked No.276 in the Fortune Top 500, and she retired at the age of 63. By Chinese law, female workers retire at the age of 50, female managers at 55, and male employees at 60. Xie studied in Qinghua University for three years before the Cultural Revolution began. She started as a technician in Bao Steel and finally became the "Wheelwoman of the Steel Carrier." Xie is a short, plain, low-key and a good drinker, her neutral look, short hair and deep voice made it difficult for people to distinguish her gender. However, she is the "Steel Woman," one of the most powerful women in the world as nominated by *Fortune* Magazine, and she has led Bao Steel to continuous growth. In 2006, SASAC invited her back at the age of 67 to run a newly established SOE.

Wu Shihong was a legend at MNC; she was the "Queen of Employees" as a professional manager. Wu belonged to the lost generation who missed out on a proper formal education during the Cultural Revolution. She was a nurse and studied English by herself before getting a job as a tea-lady at IBM in 1986. She was discriminated against and humiliated as a blue-collar worker in the early years, and she worked extremely hard to become the star salesperson at IBM. She was promoted to be General Manager of IBM in Southern China and was called the "Empress of the South." She then succeeded to the position of CEO of Microsoft China in 1998, the first mainland Chinese in this position.

Wu left Microsoft one year later and joined a large CPC, TCL, for another three years. She finally left the business field in 2002. She now lives a life of leisure and translates Western books. As a woman, probably, it is the time for her to start to enjoy her life.

difficult to survive in the Chinese culture, as the "glass ceiling" is tough and clearly visible to all.

Some foreigners at MNCs find that their female colleagues are much more open and easier to communicate and work with. In effect, given the culture of the "Superior Official," many top Chinese male graduates would take as their first choice a career at a government department or a SOE. However, the top female graduates would find it less welcoming in those two sectors. Therefore, many female talents go to MNCs where they are more appreciated and have more opportunities. The end result is that one is likely to find more male talents in the SOEs, and female talents in the MNCs.

Part II
Rising to the Challenge – Making it Happen

6
Communicating with the Chinese

Arguably the leader's most important job is to communicate. In this chapter we will look at the nature of communication in China, then examine how an outsider can start "playing the game." Warning: ditch all those Western preconceptions that good communication is about clarity, "not beating about the bush" and so on. This is an excellent precept in the West – and one we try and follow in this book. But try it in China, and you will be gazed at in pitying incomprehension. Westerners should understand the literary and philosophical traditions behind how and why the Chinese communicate in a particular way. Table 6.1 summarizes some of the key different attitudes between Westerners and the Chinese.

At the same time, don't assume that all Chinese know by some kind of magic how to communicate with each other. Communications skills are among the most popular training topics in China (especially at MNCs). It is assumed that this is to help communication between Chinese and foreigners, but actually a lot of communication issues and challenges arise amongst the Chinese themselves, inside or across departments.

As we mentioned in earlier chapters, the Chinese tend to prefer a paternalistic leader, who is expected to settle all issues. This extends to communication. It is common practice in SOEs and CPCs that department heads initiate any communication inside as well as across departments. This is frequently done informally.

This is the way to build up the platform of horizontal communication for team members internally and externally.

Western managers often see this as too "hands-on" and interfering: a "Westernized" Chinese person might feel the same. But

Table 6.1 *Key differences in attitudes of Westerners and Chinese*

Chinese view of Westerners	Westerners' view of the Chinese
Too direct and can give offence.	Unwilling to express open disagreement.
Use colloquial, unfamiliar language.	Opinions are not expressed strongly.
Dominate in meetings (which shows that they don't think the Chinese are competent).	Difficult to tell if silence and nodding mean "yes" or "no."
Difficult to tell if they are serious or joking.	Don't want to share information.
Tend to be culturally arrogant.	Don't show physical signs of urgency or excitement.
Expect a quick, simplistic response to complex questions.	

most Chinese have a need for "emotional caring" regardless of their capabilities, and a highly supportive and highly directive leader meets this need. It also explains why, when a foreign manager fully delegates and leaves the capable Chinese delegatee alone, after a while the delegatee becomes unhappy or distant.

Most expatriates are team leaders in MNCs and come from a democratic culture. They believe that it is each team member's responsibility to build up their own networks and communication channels. They are not aware that many Chinese tend to wait for their leader's approval to make a first move; many Chinese believe that even communicating with peers should be through their leader or must at least begin with some kind of acknowledgement from the leader.

CHINA: A HIGH-CONTEXT CULTURE

Westerners often object "Why won't Chinese staff tell the leader their needs?" Actually, they probably do but in a subtle way that a Chinese would pick up.

The issue at stake here is the level of context.

Every language comes with a different parcel of hidden assumptions, references, expectations – a parcel usefully referred to as subtext. We look at the surface of what is communicated and unconsciously attach our own subtexts (cultural and personal) to it, rather than the ones intended by the speaker.

However, some cultures use more subtext than others. This difference is captured in the concept of "high-context versus low-context." In high-context cultures, such as in China, there is a great deal of subtext. Communication depends on the context or nonverbal aspect of communication, i.e. interpreting what is meant rather than what is actually said. It has the following characteristics:

- What is unsaid but understood carries more weight than the verbal (or written).

- Social trust needs to precede agreement.

- Agreements are made on the basis of general trust.

- Negotiations are slow and ritualistic.

- Relationships and goodwill are highly valued.

In low-context cultures, such as most Western ones, communication depends more on explicit, expressed content and has the following characteristics:

- Interpretation depends on what is actually said or written.

- Expertise and performance are valued above reputation or connections.

- Legal contracts are necessary and binding.

- Relationships are not a priority.

- Negotiations are expected to be quick and efficient. Why waste time?

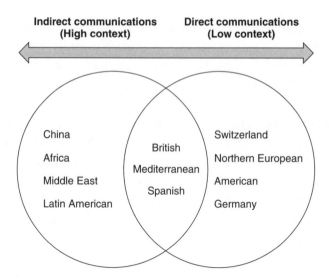

Figure 6.1 *High-context and low-context communications*
(Based on information drawn from Hall, E. T. (1976) *Beyond Culture*)

Figure 6.1 illustrates the continuum for the different cultures of the world between high- and low-context communication patterns. The continuum illustrates the potential disaster scenarios that may occur. People in high-context cultures such as China expect others to decode gestures and unarticulated moods and tones. A person from a low-context country perceives this expectation as mysterious and even perhaps underhand.

So what does one do, coming from a low-context culture to a high-context one?

Set the context first. The Chinese will present all the factors of a situation: the background, any side-issues and so on, and only then give their own personal views or recommendations. This sequence of "Because...therefore..." is the normal structure of everyday Chinese communication.

In the first ("because") stage, the context will be set up. This will include praise for various people involved in whatever it has taken to get things to the point they are now (even if such people will play no further role in the proceedings). It will also cover current issues. The objective of the speaker is to ensure that all points of view are taken into account, and hopefully thus minimize any obvious disagreements and loss of face.

In the second ("therefore") stage, recommendations are made. The Chinese speaker will still stress mutual benefits and strive for some uniform approach; if things have been done badly in the past, they will say things like "We need improvements in the area of...," rather than come out with outright criticism.

In contrast, in low-context cultures the sequence is the opposite. People are more likely to fire in the recommendations first, then follow up with the reason.

Behind this lies a fundamental difference of approach: for the Chinese, communication is about building relationships, while in the West it is about efficient exchange of information and getting things done as quickly as possible.

Chinese communication is all about keeping all parties in balance. This includes balancing the emotional and rational aspects of any communication. The emotional part plays the key role in Chinese communication. (The truth is that people everywhere make things happen based on their feelings.)

Customize each message for its recipient. "Focus on facts and ignore subjective stuff about the person you are talking to" is hardly ever an effective motto for communicating in China. Instead ask, "How will this recipient perceive the message given his/her position, personal interest, background and personality?"

Here are some bullet points to help you across the high-context/low-context divide:

- Communicate with one person at a time.

- Build rapport and two-way interaction.

- Show sincerity and an open mind.

- Listen first, then talk.

- Show your interest in others' ideas.

- Talk about the area the listener is good at or interested in, and give him/her the chance to teach you. (Chinese always like to teach others.)

- Be sensitive and respond to emotions.

- Check misunderstanding: "So what you're saying is..."

- Elaborate the pros and cons of your offer.

- Focus on others' benefits.

- Show your emotions and concern for others.

- Show your trust and support.

- Always use positive words.

- Always find something in others true to praise (if nothing else, you can pass compliment on their dress sense or hairstyle, this is acceptable in China).

- If negotiations get stuck with both parties insisting on their position, try to change the subject and find another time to communicate.

Chinese people tend to be very open about marriage, age, salary, and love to talk about children. But be very careful about addressing religion, politics or joking about the dark side of Chinese culture.

We Chinese can be very critical and open about our own culture and behavior – but only with other Chinese. It's "face" rather than ethnocentrism or nationalism that makes us so sensitive to criticism and sneers from foreigners. It is the same with our families: Chinese parents can criticize their children severely, but they won't accept outsiders saying a single negative word about their children.

RANK

China is also a country with high "power-distance," unlike the democratically minded West. Power and rank suffuse all aspects of Chinese life. As we have seen, looking at the teachings of Confucius, this isn't just about exploitation but about paternalism and taking responsibility for others rather than just "looking after number one."

Memories of the egalitarian rhetoric and appearances of the Mao era may blind Westerners to this fact. This is a great illusion (and always was). Bluntly, there is no "equal" communication among Chinese. To the same message from one person, their superior, their peer and their subordinate will feel totally different.

Let us consider the basic Confucian "rank positions" in Chinese life as shown in Figure 6.2.

For each of these, there is a different set of appropriate communication styles.

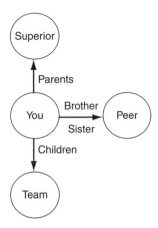

Figure 6.2 *Confucian rank positions*

Communicating with a superior (i.e., as with your parents)

- Show your respect for him or her and his or her authority in a relaxed manner.

- Don't disagree with him/her in front of others. Privately, find a point to agree first, and then talk about your ideas.

- When putting forward your ideas, do so in a tone of getting his/her advice.

- Don't immediately turn down a task you are not able to do. Say, "Let me think about it," and find a convincing reason to decline later.

- Self-blame first for any failure.

- In a case of ongoing disagreement, you may express that you would do it in your leader's way out of respect, but you keep your ideas to yourself, though you would appreciate it if he/she could further consider it. Or, if you are really sure your way is the best, find a trusted peer to influence your superior.

Communicating with a peer (your brothers or sisters)

- Be open and friendly.

- Offer your help or effort first.

- Be upfront in a polite way.

- Don't mislead by overpromising.

- Have a sense of humor – aimed at yourself.

- Chat.

- If you make a mistake, say "sorry" openly.

- Keep him/her informed of all relevant information.

- In conflict, talk directly to each other first in a casual environment.

- Don't say bad things about your superior.

Communicating with team members (your children)

- Encourage them to talk more.

- Be patient and warm up the conversation.

- Listen carefully to their emotion and intention.

- Show your trust and understanding emotionally.

- Talk about strengths first, then about areas where they need to improve.

- Be authentic and honest, using their language.

- Offer tangible help you can deliver: don't agree to or promise anything you are not sure of.

- In disagreement, be assertive and confronting in a nice way. If he/she is very emotional, let him/her get it out, then go back to your standpoint. Or find another time to continue the discussion.

- In an ongoing disagreement, arrange for one of his/her trusted peers to influence them.

In all these areas, be yourself, and try your best to understand your team members' needs and emotions, which will vary according to their generation and background.

Most important of all, try to understand as much as you can about Chinese culture. This isn't just an optional extra, like taking a bus trip round the local tourist sites; this is the royal road to building respectful relationships with your Chinese colleagues. Never forget that behind their apparently cold exteriors, the Chinese are very sensitive!

To conclude, here are some basic tips for communicating with Chinese people, in all contexts.

- Start by understanding the Chinese view that relationship-building is key to breaking down barriers, and that this takes time.

- In the initial stages of any contact, formality rules. Address the leader first (and keep talking to the leader throughout if you are dealing with an SOE).

- Address people by their titles.

- Frankness is almost always considered rude. Be subtle.

- If you ask a question and get either no answer or an oblique response, don't push the point. Approach the person later, in private.

- Don't criticize an individual in front of others.

- Silence does not mean your message is not getting through. The wise Confucian is expected to listen in silence.

- Remember that if a senior manager is present, junior staff will not speak.

- The Chinese are much more reserved when it comes to expressing emotions than their Western counterparts.

- Laughter is often a sign of hiding embarrassment or discomfort. Don't take offence: it is a defensive posture, a way to save face.

- Chinese make less eye contact than Westerners. This is a matter of degree: you should still make some eye contact. But not too much, and don't expect too much back.

- Physical contact should be restricted to handshakes: American-style backslapping does not go down well.

Yvonne was an English expatriate, and the National Sales and Marketing Manager of a Joint Venture based in Beijing. She reported to the Managing Director, who was British, and the Deputy Managing Director, who was a Chinese. She had five Chinese colleagues reporting directly to her. Yvonne worked very hard and travelled around the country to help build up the local sales teams. She was outgoing, energetic, and direct. She had good relationships with her peers as well as the local sales teams.

Yvonne's office was next to both the Managing Director's office and Deputy Managing Director's office. Apart from saying hello every morning, she occasionally talked with the Managing Director when she needed help. She often directly spoke out in the department heads' meeting as most of her Chinese peers were quiet. She hardly talked to the Deputy Managing Director as she did not need his help on a specific task; also, she thought that he might not feel comfortable to chat in a second language. However, the Deputy Managing Director was quite annoyed as he thought Yvonne did not respect him.

Yvonne liked one of her directly reporting colleagues, Maria, who was very capable, and Yvonne delegated to Maria and left her alone most of time to complete her tasks. Maria was an emotional person, when she was under pressure, she found it difficult to keep to herself. Maria felt that Yvonne just took her hard work for granted.

When contract review time came around for Yvonne, she could not get her contract renewed as she was evaluated as not capable of leading the team to perform.

The point to make here is that communication is critical even if it's not work-related, because of face, respect and harmony. Communication conveys these essential core values, therefore Yvonne's actions were perceived to be snobbish or arrogant to the Chinese Deputy Managing Director; and to Maria she appeared to be dismissive. These are both serious *faux pas* in the Chinese context.

7
Leading Teams

MANAGEMENT LEVELS

Zeng Shiqiang, a popular Chinese leadership and management thinker, says that the most effective way to lead Chinese teams is to apply the right philosophy for the right level of staff.

He goes on to say that the relationship of senior, middle and lower management is like the traditional philosophical relationship between Heaven, Human, and Earth. Senior management is "Heaven": it is way above, powerful, mysterious, changeable and unpredictable. Lower management is "Earth": it produces necessities for the organization to live; it is stable, reachable, unplowed fertile soil. Middle Management is the "Human" link between these two things: it is the factor that makes the organization survive and thrive. A crucial point to understand is that these three layers are equally important.

Daoism is for senior management; Confucianism is for middle management; Mohism is for lower management. We would argue that Militarism and Legalism can also contribute to some degree, and summarize this in figure 7.1.

SENIOR MANAGEMENT

In China, it doesn't matter who you are, once you have entered this league, your position will bring you respect and compliance from people below you.

Figure 7.1 *Application of leadership theories*

As such a manager, it is better to lead by applying Naturalistic Theory coupled with Strategic Theory in the following way:

- Delegate as much as possible.

- Leave middle management their own autonomies; don't interfere with their daily management.

- Acknowledge team achievement, be invisible in a success.

- Implement stable policies and minimize change of rules.

- Convey organizational strategy clearly to the team.

- Share your knowledge of external environments with the team.

- Keep a low profile.

- Maintain a friendly, modest and accessible image in public.

- Always be calm.

- Be caring.

- Give face to anyone reporting to you: praise in public and criticize in private.

- Use coaching to help their self-development.

- Consult your team before making a major decision.

- Be assertive and stick to major decisions.

- Supervise middle management teams from a distance.

- Be insightful of any movements in the organization

By all means talk to lower-level staff to show your accessibility, but be aware that it is better to avoid private talk in public with groups of them, as this may upset or worry your middle management, who will probably think you are "checking them out."

MIDDLE MANAGEMENT

This is the backbone of an organization, and thus under huge pressure. They may have to play "face off" to make senior management happy and to make lower management deliver; experiencing extremes from double support to double pronged attacks is their daily life.

For this level, applying Humane Theory is probably a sensible choice, but not the only one. The challenge many Chinese organizations face is low productivity, and one of the key reasons for this is that internal regulations are either incomplete or not being executed strictly. Thus, the exercise of Institutional Theory would benefit both organization and individual.

However, Humane Theory focuses on people, morality and ethics, while Institutional Theory focuses on regulations, legislation and policy. To integrate these two contradicting theories and maintain balance is a big challenge. The following principles help:

- Be a role model for both types of management, institutional and humane.

- Care about the team's feelings and personal issues.

- Help team members set up SMART goals.

- Track their progress towards these.

- Set up clear rules, working processes, and incentive schemes.

- Get consensus from the team.

- Create a coaching culture.

- Don't be hands-off: direct and support team members.

- Educate staff if rules are broken. If punishment is necessary, tell them privately and don't shame them.

LOWER MANAGEMENT

Lower management has to lead the blue-collar workers, who can be very powerful, like water that "can make the boat sail and also make the boat sink." Making a living is probably the fundamental drive for these people, so to focus on their personal welfare is the key to stabilizing the team and making it perform. As a result, a team leader may find it appropriate to exercise Altruistic Theory in the following way:

- Work and live with the team, be an "intimate brother/sister" rather than a leader.

- Strive for team members' personal benefit, which is superior to yours.

- Care about team members' family issues.

- Help them achieve business goals by working with them.

- Socialize with them and their family members.

- Be decisive and take responsibility if things go wrong.

- Protect the team and stand by them.

- Be assertive and strict on organizational policy and implement it like a domestic discipline.

TEAM DYNAMICS

In theory, as the Chinese are collective-oriented, team working should be easier than in an "individual-oriented" culture. But actually, teamwork is one of the biggest challenges for managers in China, and there is huge demand in the training market for techniques of teambuilding. This is because Chinese teamwork requires a strong leader.

"One Chinese is a dragon; a group of Chinese is a worm" is an old saying – and still relevant today. Given the culture of "filial piety," hierarchy and respecting authority, a "parent" is a psychological prerequisite for Chinese team members to have a sense of belonging. They expect protection and give loyalty in return. It is common in SOEs and CPCs for people to confide their personal or family issues to the leader. A "parenthood or brotherhood" team leader can be very powerful in a CPC; they can easily take the whole team away when they quit the company. Mo Zi's "code of brotherhood" still prevails among less-educated Chinese.

Hence, teamwork is determined by the legitimate team leader, who is the soul and catalyst of the team. He/she needs to be the "dragon heart" to compose all team members into a "dragon" by balancing individuals' personal interests and functions. Without such a leader, each individual will drift to his/her own direction, and the team will be a useless "worm."

In Belbin's team model, the role of leadership is not necessarily only exercised by the team leader. However, in China, this role is expected to be played exclusively by the team leader. Otherwise, people will lose respect for the leader and will accuse the other person playing a leadership role of exceeding their authority – a crime we shall say more about shortly.

It is important to bear in mind two things to lead Chinese teams or in the process of any people dynamics namely face and *guānxì*, which have been discussed extensively in Chapter 3. Once team roles have been set out, the family model discussed in the previous chapter becomes highly relevant.

TEAM MOTIVATION

In the general day-to-day motivation of a Chinese team...

- Talk to team members frequently.

- Show your "human touch"; care about them as individuals and look after their families.

- Give public recognition and praise.

- Show your trust and appreciation.

- Lead by example.

- Plan their career path and personal development with them.

- Celebrate success and bear loss together with the team.

- Apply reward and punishment in a flexible and balanced way, depending on the situation and the needs of the individual.

- Criticism and provocation can be effective for certain types of people, the task-driven extraverts. It is quite common for people working in SOEs to take leader's criticism as motivation, as that means attention from the leader.

Salary is important, of course, but for people at managerial level it will not make up for a leader's failure to carry out the above. If your Chinese manager asks for an unreasonable pay rise, it is likely that he/she has been demotivated by nonfinancial factors. This also creates a way out of an impasse – you

Mark is an expatriate Marketing Manager at an MNC, he has six Chinese colleagues reporting directly to him. Rachel is his favorite as she is very enthusiastic, energetic, hardworking, and speaks very good English, and Mark feels it's very easy to communicate with her and it's Rachel who understands him best in the team.

Compared with other team members, Mark spends more time with Rachel for social talks. During team meetings, he begins to realize that Rachel is the one talking most: the other team members are talking less and less.

Mark tries to talk with other team members as much as he can, but they do not seem to be interested in talking to him; they just do what they have to do, unlike Rachel who takes the initiative to make things happen.

At the year-end appraisal, Mark gives the highest bonus to Rachel as she organized several promotional events successfully. However, Rachel is unhappy as she is isolated by the others, she finds it difficult to do things as she cannot get her colleagues' support.

Mark received resignation letters from two team members who felt the appraisal was unfair. Only one team member seemed to be comfortable with her appraisal – and Mark had been trying to get rid of her as she was lazy and incapable.

Mark could prevent this situation arising by taking the following actions:

Mark should:

- Recognize Rachel's contribution privately.

- Coach Rachel to help others.

- Talk to other team members more during the coffee time.

- Encourage other team members to talk more in meetings.

- Not show favor towards Rachel in front of others.

- Clarify the position with team members about their bonus-related target.

can refuse the request, and they can resign without anyone losing face.

Reasonable Unfairness

> Reasonable unfairness is an effective way to motivate Chinese... Because unfairness is everywhere, the only way is to continuously improve yourself to get better treatment from your leader.
>
> Zeng Shiqiang

Fairness is an essential clause in the "psychological contract" in the Western workplace. In China, however, people value "reasonable" more than "fair." People acknowledge there is no absolute fairness; what they need is a good reason to accept unfairness. Hence the concept of "reasonable unfairness" in the quote above. What constitutes a "good reason" can be defined differently in various contexts.

It is "reasonable unfairness" to promote one of three equally capable employees on the grounds that the promoted person is "oldest" at an SOE, "most trusted by the leader" at a CPC, and "hardest worker" at an MNC. But by contrast, unreasonable causes for such a promotion would be "newcomer" at SOEs, "challenges authority" at a CPC, and the "foreigner's favorite" at an MNC.

CONCLUSION

Teamwork is a key to organizational success in China, but to build a high-performance team is extremely challenging, as it requires a lot from the team leader. Such a person should ideally be a Confucian *jūnzǐ*, a role model of wisdom, energy, dedication and self-sacrifice.

The hierarchical and bureaucratic models of most Chinese businesses make it hard to prosper by these values, but if you can achieve it, it is definitely the best way to lead.

As Confucius understood 2,500 years ago, leadership is essentially an emotional business. Emotional resonance with a role model is the most powerful form of leadership in China. Probably in the rest of the world, too, though rational Westerners may be unwilling to admit the fact.

8
Delegation and Decision Making

DELEGATION

This is a daily practice for Western managers. In China, the story is very different.

The start of a new relationship in China is marked by distrust or, at best, cautious trust – as in the Chinese legal system, where the accused is assumed guilty and has to prove his or her innocence. In general, people tend to accept the authority of the position rather than the person holding that position: this is especially so at SOEs. The presidents of many business units or functions in SOEs tend to take full responsibility for all cases, therefore most Chinese managers do not delegate authority.

They need to ask themselves three crucial questions before they delegate:

1. "If I delegate my authority to others, will people still respect and listen to me?"

2. "Can I trust the one to whom I want to delegate? Has this person proved that he/she is trustworthy on everything?"

3. "If something happened, can I bear the loss of taking full responsibility?"

There are numerous negative lessons in Chinese history. In feudal times, the classic disastrous piece of delegation happened when the emperor delegated to his officials who then defied him and started rebellions. And not long ago, Mao delegated his power to the Gang of Four when he was physically incapable of leading the country, and they plunged China into the abyss of the Cultural Revolution.

On the other hand, from delegatee's point of view, he or she would worry about how to exercise the authority in a way that steers a correct path between two unforgivable sins by Chinese standards, which are:

1. Failure to fulfill one's duty; this may make one lose one's job or position.

2. Exceeding one's authority; this is seen as being even worse.

Here is a classic story.

> Two thousand five hundred years ago, the King of Han State was a reputable ruler who governed his state well with rigorous rules. Two of his officials were the Steward of the Royal Blanket and the Steward of the Royal Hat, who were delegated to look after the King's blanket and hats respectively. One night, the King got drunk and fell asleep without covering himself. The Steward of the Royal Blanket was away, but the Steward of the Royal Hat was worried that the King would catch a cold, so covered the King with a blanket.
>
> The King awoke, noticed the blanket, and then found out from the servants what had happened.
>
> The Steward of the Royal Blanket was demoted, because he didn't fulfill his duty. However, the Steward of the Royal Hat was executed, because he exceeded his authority by handling the blanket.

Much as this sounds like a rather unpleasant fairy tale, it is actually true. Stranger still (to Western readers, brought up with beliefs about "taking initiative"), many Chinese still think the King did the right thing.

When authority is threatened, people tend to become Legalists rather than Confucians. Not surprisingly, Chinese people are ambivalent about both delegating and being delegated to.

The common practice in Chinese organizations is for the senior manager to hold the authority, the middle manager to take responsibility and the employee to claim the benefit. Thus, delegation occurs mainly from senior management to middle management, but both parties have to make tremendous efforts to make it happen.

Let's explore the two dimensions that lead to effective delegation:

The Art of Delegating

If you follow the points below, you are ready to delegate in China:

Do:

- Delegate to only a few people who are truly capable and trustworthy.

- Take time to assess informally whether the person you want to delegate to is such a person.

- Hold on to most of your authority: only delegate a small part of your authority, which will not irreparably damage you if things go badly wrong.

- Check occasionally and irregularly on progress. The delegatee will feel cared for but not distrusted. And if the delegatee plays tricks, he/she won't be able to fool you as he/she doesn't know your routine.

- Inform others in the meeting to whom and what you delegate. It gives legitimacy to the delegatee who can get support from other members.

- Change the people to whom you delegate if the situation changes.

- Trust those delegatees who don't exceed their authority.

Don't:

- Delegate to anyone you have doubts about.

- Doubt the one to whom you have delegated.

- Show favor to the delegatee in front of others – they may feel jealous.

- Interfere with the delegatee's work.

- Listen to anyone who slanders the one you have delegated.

- Trust delegatees who exceed their authority.

The Art of Receiving Delegation

Middle managers are in the toughest position; they are most delegated to and also suspected of both contending with senior management and taking advantage of employees.

To get delegated to, implement the following strategies:

- Follow the tenet of Naturalistic Theory that "no one will fight the one who does not fight." People tend to delegate to the one who doesn't fight. Never ask for delegation. If you are delegated to, your first reaction should be to decline the authority but take the task and responsibility; if you do this, your superior won't feel any threat that you intend to take over his/her position.

- Build rapport with your superior; listen to his or her emotions and intentions. Don't expect clear instruction on how much authority has been delegated to you, as your superior needs leeway if something happens out of your control.

- Report to your superior periodically, and check your decisions with him or her before you execute in order to dispel any worry about your coveting authority (also in case changes have been made at a senior level that affect the context of the decision).

- Take delegation as an honor and keep low key in front of others. Delegation is the most precious thing to have; it is the highest form of recognition. But if you flaunt it, you will not get the team's support, and without this support you will fail.

- Understand that the delegatee is not necessarily the most capable, but the person most trusted by the leader.

In view of the above, hopefully, you will realize how much of a challenge delegation is for Chinese managers. It requires high EQ for both parties to make delegation happen and work.

DECISION MAKING

Chinese tend to take a longer time to make decisions than Westerners. This isn't indecisiveness but holistic thinking. In the West, most decisions are made to achieve a specific goal, whereas in China the principle of decision making is "the balance of all parties." Chinese decision makers will think through the impact on all related *guānxì*. There is also a Chinese focus on the tendency of situations to change – which, of course, goes back to the *Yi Jing*. A sense that the future is uncertain underlies much Chinese decision making.

During the process of decision making, the following questions occur all the time;

- "Who initiated this?"

- "Who will benefit most/least?"

- "Who might disagree with it or be upset by it?"

- "Who will be recognized if it succeeds?"

- "Who will be blamed or lose face if it fails?"

- "What will the situation be like when the decision is made to execute?"

- "What will the environment be like by then?"

Scenario 1:

Mr. Wei – the boss
Mr. Zhang – Sales Manager
(Mr. Wei likes and trusts Mr. Zhang, he sees Mr. Zhang as his right-hand man)

> Wei: Little Zhang, you are delegated to make decision on this business project as I trust you.
> Zhang: Thanks, that's great.

(Zhang is having a meeting with one of his customers in the meeting room, Wei is walking past and overhears.)

> Customer: Can you make a decision on this?
> Zhang: Yes.
> Customer: Are you sure you don't need to check with your boss?
> Zhang: It's not necessary, I can make this decision on my own.

(They shake hands and Zhang signs the contract.)

(Zhang comes back to his office; he is asked to see Wei in his office.)

> Wei: I have decided not to delegate to you anymore.
> Zhang: What's wrong with me?
> Wei: I don't mind delegating to you, but if you swindle and bluff, the company will incur a huge loss.

Question: What do you think happened here? Try to answer this before you look at Scenario 2, which gives you an insight into what Zhang did wrong.

Scenario 2:

Wei: Little Zhang, you are delegated to make decision on this business project as I trust you.

Zhang: Thanks for trusting me, but you don't need to delegate. I will be responsible for this. I believe you are the right person to make the decision.

(Zhang is having a meeting with one of his customers in the meeting room, Wei is walking past and overhears.)

Customer: Can you make a decision on this?

Zhang: I believe that my boss would agree with me, but I would like to report to him first.

Customer: Oh, but I don't have much time to spare.

Zhang: Don't worry, just give me few minutes, I am sure he is around, I would like to introduce you to him.

(Wei quickly walks back to his office. Soon Zhang knocks his door.)

Wei: Come in please.

Zhang: Hi, boss, the customer is here, I told him we'd love to offer the service, and I proposed the plan which I discussed with you last week, he is quite satisfied. I think we can sign the contract now. Do you agree?

Wei: (*Very supportive*) Of course, it is up to you, I have delegated you to conduct the business.

Zhang: The customer is here, would you please come to sign the contract, and I would like to introduce you to him. Do you have a few minutes?

Wei: (*Smiling and pats Zhang's shoulders*) Definitely, let's go. Also, you sign the contract, you are the person in charge.

Thus, a decision may take a tremendously long time, and be implemented in as flexible a way as possible. This is the typical process in SOEs and CPCs.

In MNCs, things are a bit different. Although the culture of MNCs is mainly goal-directed and linear-thinking, foreign and Westernized Chinese managers can encounter resistance from Chinese colleagues about their neglect of *guānxì* and of changing situations.

In SOEs normally several senior managers jointly make decisions at functional level and above, while middle management needs to coordinate and influence each of them for a final decision. In CPCs, senior management, mainly the CEO, make all the decisions; the process is shorter as middle managers only deal with one or two senior members. The quickest process is in MNCs. Here middle management is delegated to make final decision, to some extent, at least.

It is common practice at SOEs and CPCs for the real decision maker not to be present at business meetings, this is in order to prevent any loss of face should there be any disagreements or the need to say "No" to a proposal. These meetings are normally conducted by those at a level below the final decision makers. The final decision makers are only involved when the deal is done.

Getting Decisions in China

Some expatriates are always puzzled that their Chinese counterparts are very polite but not clear about their intentions. This means a decision is still being made.

Some time later, they may receive overwhelming hospitality, and conclude that things are going well. This may not be the case: hospitality towards guests is a key Confucian tenet.

They may never actually be told the decision, if it is "no." Chinese people do not like to tell you "no," as this involves disharmony and loss of face all round. Usually some circumlocution is produced – for example the classic bureaucrats' "It is not convenient at the moment."

Only if you hear "OK, it's a deal!" can you assume a "yes." At which point, the negotiations may just be about to start...

In March 2008, a Norwegian University attended a bidding meeting for technical training for a large SOE and submitted their proposal.

In April, they were informed that the HR Director of this SOE would like to visit their campus; they were very excited and believed that they were likely to get the contract.

In June, when they thought the SOE might consider another supplier, The HR Director came to visit their campus, who was happy with their facilities. They were told that they would like to have further meetings on program details.

In August, the university was puzzled as to whether the deal was going to happen. They were informed that the Training Manager, who reported directly to the SOE Director of HR wanted to have a meeting in Beijing.

In September, they had a meeting with the Training Manager and Training Coordinator, they were told that their program was fine but the price was too high.

They had not overcharged and they could not cut the price, so they thought they had wasted their time on this deal and they decided to forget about it.

In March of the following year, they were informed that this SOE decided to send their first delegation of 30 people to come over in June. The university was taken by surprise: they did not have enough time to organize the program and they were not able to accommodate such a large number of people at such short notice.

The moral of this story is that the Chinese always like to bargain on price, it is part of the Chinese business mindset, so you should always be prepared to make a concession on price to get the goodwill. Sometimes, they don't necessarily expect you to cut down, but they will make an attempt to bargain on this point. Finally, decisions take time to be reached by SOEs.

A British software company was seeking a local partner in China to promote their new software. They were introduced to a Chinese agent by a Chinese person working for the DTI. They met this agent in the hotel they lived in, and they were impressed with her open mind and professional experience.

The agent told them that the market here in China was very competitive; however, there was still a chance for their software product. She would like to work with them, but she needed financial support initially for promoting this product through her connections, which was approximately $8,000 a year.

In the meantime, they were invited by a SOE to talk about collaboration. They visited the SOE's huge office and they were given a big Chinese banquet and enjoyed the Chinese food very much. They had a pleasant meeting, they gave a presentation of their products, and their Chinese hosts listened and smiled all the time, and seemed very interested in this business. They did not talk about specific plans and budgets.

They were overwhelmed by the SOE's hospitality, and they assumed that the partnership was established and their products would be in the Chinese market soon. They decided to work with this SOE as they thought this big company was in a better position than that agent to win the market.

One month after they came back to Britain, they tried to sign a contract with the SOE but were told it was in the process. Although they pushed several times, nothing happened for a year. Eventually, they realized what they encountered was just a normal "Welcome foreign guest protocol" at SOEs.

They tried to get the agent back, and she declined and said she had another partner to work with, and brought that partner $2 million a year worth of business

The moral here is don't be taken in by the lavish banquets and welcomes, it is part of the Chinese protocol. Secondly, do not be fooled by the size of the company because success is through individual connections or *guānxì*.

9
Negotiations

Behind the concern for harmony and the extensive Confucian hospitality, the Chinese are amongst the toughest negotiators in the world. Many have learnt this in childhood, bargaining in shops or at market stalls: China is still an agrarian society at heart. China is also a society that was once poor: in the old days, every "fen" saved was important, and this mindset lives on, reflected in the detail to which negotiation is taken.

However, alongside this, the old concern for face, hierarchy and the welfare of the group remain an essential part of the mix. This means that Chinese negotiators will also focus on means and process. The correct way of proceeding will matter hugely, and the decision, however tightly it may seem to have been negotiated, will ultimately be an emotional one.

This book may be accused of accepting some of the Western "China experts" writings which accuse the Chinese of deceptive, manipulative negotiating tactics and so on. Some Chinese writers would argue this is all speculative. We take the position that the Western perception just described is due to misunderstanding and not knowing the differences between Chinese and Western negotiating philosophies. It is the aim of this section to outline these differences and show that the negotiating philosophies are very much tied in with the Chinese core values and leadership philosophies as outlined in the previous chapters. The Western negotiator needs to understand the broader context of Chinese culture and values.

Educated Chinese have studied from childhood two classic Chinese texts, *The Art of War* by Sun Zi and *The 36 Strategies*. For Western negotiators to enter China without some knowledge of these two books is like walking into a battlefield without ammunition.

The Art of War by Sun Zi was written over 2,000 years ago. Its most important message is the importance of outwitting your opponent. Not just via surprise – though this is a key aspect of Sun Zi's philosophy – but by subtly manipulating the enemy to do what you need them to do in order to put them at the maximum disadvantage.

One key to achieving this is the acquisition of information: the best-informed side usually wins. Of particular use is information about the character of the opposing general, especially any weaknesses, on which you must play. If he is impetuous, offer him the chance to do something rash; if he is cowardly, attack; if he is obsessed with honor, insult him (and so on).

Another key to manipulation is deceit. The more you can fool the enemy about your character, numbers, strengths, intentions and so on, the further ahead you are of them in the mental battle that is strategy. Ideally, you should fool the enemy into thinking you are being manipulated by them, but actually you are in charge. You should perpetually change your methods and plans "making it impossible for others to anticipate your purpose." As Sun Zi wrote, "All warfare is based on deception."

The Chinese always think strategically. If they appear to be avoiding specifics and remaining general, this is not an attempt to avoid the issues but a natural consequence of their approach. Here is a story that we would like to share with you to illustrate strategic thinking. Chinese stories often involve clever strategic ploys. This story dates, as many such stories do, from the Warring States era (476–221 BC). This was a time of perpetual conflict. It was the golden age of classical Chinese strategy – though it was probably not much fun to live in, unless you were a general.

General Tian of the Kingdom of Qi would race horses with the prince of Qi as a hobby. The usual procedure was to have three races, and the traditional approach of the General was to pit his best, middle and worst horses against similar horses of the prince. One day, however, General Tian approached his master strategist for advice, and the strategist recommended that he should race his worst horse against the prince's best, pit his best horse against his rival's middle one, and then use his middle horse to compete against his rival's worst. This advice was followed, the General won two races and lost one, and was declared the overall winner of the contest.

This story beautifully illustrates the Chinese mindset of looking at situations not in absolute but in relative terms. The prince of Qi was happy for the General because he won the contest, and he was satisfied because his best horse won his race and his "face" was saved.

So one needs to look at the bigger picture when negotiating with the Chinese, and not just on specifics of a contract.

Still looking forward to your next meeting?

The 36 Strategies was compiled after the time of Sun Zi, but not long after; it uses some of his ideas, nobody knows who the author was. The strategies are grouped under six main categories, three for attack and three for defense.

The three types of attack strategy are:

- Advantageous strategies, for use when you have a numerical or other advantage.

- Opportunistic strategies.

- Offensive strategies, about decisive actions.

For defense they are:

- Creating confusion in the enemy.

- Deception strategies.

- "Desperate strategies" for when things have clearly gone wrong.

We would like to illustrate how some of these strategies work in a negotiating context.

One of the strategies is called "Conserving energy while the enemy tires himself out," used when there is no urgency to rush the deal and when time and resources are to your advantage. You have no need to make a direct attack: sit and watch your adversaries as they blunder round. Try to lead them up as many blind alleys as possible, a bit like a tennis player putting the ball in alternate far corners of the court. The final strike can then be quick and simple. There are many historical examples to illustrate this strategy (in the West, it was used by the Roman general Fabius to vanquish the previously unbeatable Hannibal).

This "wait and see tactic" is frequently used by Chinese negotiators. Regular negotiators in China will be familiar with this scenario: today the Chinese company wants to see a detailed plan for production. Tomorrow they ask for clarification and time to discuss the matter further. The following day, they make a request to revisit the production plant with a senior manager from their side. Meanwhile the potential foreign company is eager to sign the deal. Head office is getting impatient. "All we need is the Chinese signature," say the Western negotiators. The Chinese want to discuss more details...

The Western company has put itself at a disadvantage by its haste. Maybe it has a notion of gaining a "first mover advantage" – a most dubious benefit, especially when the Chinese, who have read their Sun Zi and their *36 Strategies*, know that the company is desperate for it and can thus be manipulated via that desire. (Arguably "first mover" is a weak strategy even if not played upon: Chinese companies are now advancing on early Western entrants in areas such as mobile phones and white goods.)

Deception in business can take many forms. Chinese may play at being innocent and ask for more and more information on your product. As consultants, we have been asked for detailed outlines of our report "just so we can see what we are getting." What they meant was "so we can photocopy them and use them while telling you we're buying from someone else." How do you get round that? You have to trust your intermediary. You must also establish in your own mind how much you are prepared to give. But remember too that you are at the start of a relationship, even though these guys are currently trying to pull wool over your eyes. Get to know them. If you can, offer them an invitation to the West. Court them.

Note that your competitors will probably be doing the same: in the end it will boil down to whether the company you are courting likes you more than the others. Yes, this is a long process, but it is how business in China works.

Another ploy is secrecy, which can be used quite effectively by the Chinese in many negotiations. When you ask them for details, in search of specific buying signals – "What is it that you are really looking for?" – you will get vague answers. This can be – no, it always is – infuriating. Don't fall into the trap of providing ever more detail about what you offer, to the point at which it can be stolen. Just take them out to another dinner.

Don't forget that from the Chinese perspective many Western businesses are unethical in their desire to make a fast buck without wishing to spend more time developing the business relationship or understanding Chinese cultural mores.

As we have already highlighted, key, trust-based business relationships is the name of the game. Foreigners need to commit themselves to a long-term approach of developing the necessary contacts and persevering with them in the face of competition and hurdles. If you are really earnest about the relationship and loyal in sustaining it, you stand the best chance of being rewarded with equal loyalty and trust.

Another example of a strategic approach is called "Luring the tiger from its lair." Essentially what this means is that to catch a tiger it is better to lure it from its hideout in the mountains and into the urban area, which would be to its disadvantage and thus lead it to be destroyed. Applying this to business, it is best to lure your competitors out of their territory and comfort zone, and then defeat them at their weakest. This strategy is only used when a direct attack is too difficult or dangerous to undertake.

A possible example, is the way some countries in Asia such as Singapore, attract foreign talent or foreign investment by world class MNCs. So to lure the "tigers" from their home territory, they offer investment guarantees, tax holidays, incentives, supporting facilities, high-quality lifestyles, and transform their city into a major cultural and entertainment centre, etc.

When we speak with Westerners about Chinese business strategies, they can be dismissive and even rant on about how immoral some of the Chinese approach to business discussions is. What they mean is that the Chinese are not "playing ball" by Western rules; the Chinese are not easy to come to agreements with; the Chinese ask for too many details about processes, procedures and products; they repeat requests for certain items (and so on).

The upset Westerners are missing the point: these things are all part of Chinese strategic thinking. The Chinese approach all negotiations with a strategic mindset. Do not fool yourself that, because few of them have been on MBA courses or use management buzz words, they are ill equipped: on the contrary, they will have been bought up on tales of strategy. Having studied both Eastern and Western strategies, we find the Eastern approaches much more subtle than Western ones. This may be why they are perceived by Westerners as "deceptive."

Chinese companies competing with one another adopt many of the classical Chinese military strategies almost by instinct, each side being intuitively aware of the processes involved. Let us begin with the Chinese requirement for "excessive" knowledge about the Western company. This is part of a strategy to size you up and to estimate your ability to conduct a commercial battle. The Chinese are following one of Sun Zi's strategic objectives, which is to "grasp the enemy's terrain." Master Sun sums this up when he says:

> Know your enemy, know yourself, and you can fight a
> hundred battles with no danger of defeat. When you are

ignorant of the enemy but know yourself, your chances
of winning and losing are equal. If you don't know either
your enemy or yourself, you are bound to perish in all
battles.

This passage shows a clear understanding of competitive intelligence. We know today that if a company can gain information
about the strategic moves of its competitors, understand its customers and understand itself, it will gain the upper hand in the
market. In a similar fashion, the Chinese are trying to gain the
competitive advantage by understanding where the Western company is coming from. Indeed, according to Wei Wang (2006), of
the 8,550 Chinese SOEs that entered Joint Ventures in the early
1990s, about 5,000 did not even have their own asset valuation.
At the same time, the Chinese also felt that the Western companies overvalued their technology and know-how. Therefore, the
purpose of obtaining as much information as possible about the
"enemy" is to win the commercial battle before it has begun. For
Sun Zi, to win a battle by fighting is not the best strategy as it is
costly in terms of human and material resources. For him the ideal
scenario is summed up thus: ".... to subdue the enemy without
fighting is the supreme excellence."

The application of this principle of achieving victory without
conflict in business means a company must win by strategy. If you
start engaging in tactical warfare, such as cutting prices and giving
discounts, then you have not won the war but are simply skirmish-
ing. A true strategy would imply the use of an indirect approach
to sustain your competitive advantage in the market without even
confronting the competitor.

To illustrate another example of negotiating strategies at work;
China is now a "hot" market for many global companies. The
Chinese will take advantage of this fact, and would make poor
business strategists if they did not do this. Many other nations
exploit such advantages (as with the strategic use of oil resources
by some Middle Eastern countries). China is an almost irresistible
lure, with its cheap labor force and vast potential internal market:
the Chinese are bound to exploit this lure to the full. They would

be crazy not to. As Sun Zi would say: "Draw them in with the prospect of gain, take them by confusion."

The way to "take them by confusion" is to use deception strategies. These entail many tactics such as pretending not to know much about your company, appearing naïve and ignorant in the negotiation process, and using the standard approach of "in China we do things like this." In the process of appearing weak and lost, the Chinese are hoping to gain a psychological advantage over you. Sun Zi again sums it up: "One with great skill appears inept." This will make you overconfident and thus tempt you to expose your weaknesses, which will then be exploited to the full.

Please note that this is not done in a malicious tone or manner; it is part of the game to win tactical points and advantage. Indeed, most Chinese negotiators are very hospitable, polite and pleasant. You could be cynical and say this in itself is a strategic approach. You would probably be right – but remember that the Confucian rules of human interaction are at work here, too, and these are more important than any specific business transaction. Don't be too cynical – understand the rules!

This is not the end of the story

One of the first rules in negotiating in China is that signing on the dotted line is only the beginning of your negotiations, not the end of it. Be prepared to revisit your contractual obligations, detail by detail.

From the Chinese point of view, signing a piece of paper is just another step along the road of building a long, harmonious relationship. This should be understood and worked with rather than railed against. If foreign businesses understand this, they will have made a strategic leap in their thinking about the China market.

This particularly annoys Westerners, especially if the negotiations have been going on for a long time, anyway, but this is how it is, and it just has to be accepted.

Note that the "renegotiating" Chinese are very unlikely to renege on their contract; they are simply continuing to jostle for advantage. It is all part of the "war of the marketplace." Remember that Sun Zi has nothing to say about "fair" or "unfair": war and negotiation are about who has the upper hand, the best bargaining position at any given time. Sorry, but that's how it is.

PUBLIC AND PRIVATE

As in most aspects of Chinese life, there is a public and private level of operations. The public face of negotiation is what takes place in conference rooms and boardrooms, with many people involved in the process. It is this type of negotiation that is protracted and requires infinite patience. It is during such negotiations that both parties try to understand what the other party intends.

The private face of negotiations involves discussions between key individuals outside the confines of formal conference room settings. Generally, the Chinese do not appear to be direct about their objectives in formal negotiations. Sometimes negotiations can stall at this stage, and that is when you need to meet one or two members of the Chinese team on a personal level outside the formal arena.

Chinese negotiators will always deny any critical comment about their company or organization, even if they are well aware of the shortcoming. This is because they will not admit failings in front of their colleagues or in front of a foreigner. This can be a problem, especially in a sales situation, when you are looking for buying signals such as "we need more X" or "we've a problem with Y." The way round this, of course, is to build relationships with individuals. In a one-to-one context; once you have established personal relationships with particular people, they are more likely to tell you the true story.

It is in these situations, when the Chinese are relaxed, that they will open up more and more. Such occasions often centre round the sharing of food. Wise Westerners in negotiations with the Chinese familiarize themselves with the etiquette of dining in China. A wise Weterner also learns about Chinese food, and enjoys the banquets.

STATUS AND *GUĀNXÌ*

It is important to match like with like when negotiating. Chinese negotiators will take a keen interest in the authority and status of your team. Sending someone with high status will be perceived by the Chinese as showing respect to them as well as demonstrating that the negotiations are being taken seriously. If the Western firm sends someone of insufficient rank, this will be construed as a loss of face on the Chinese side. Send in senior lead negotiators, which will be seen as an honor (the right initial strategy); send in junior people if you feel you are being messed about.

Guānxì are at the heart of negotiation. Chinese participants will want, and probably expect, a level of personal relationship with their counterpart in the negotiation that Westerners would consider unnecessary and even undesirable. This expectation can be seen by some in the West as a cynical ploy to create an emotional bond and thus a more favorable attitude towards the Chinese side. This is unfair. From a Western perspective, personal friendship may be derived from a business relationship: the Chinese prefer things the other way round. Establish relationships as a basis for business deals; build ties that extend beyond the negotiation table.

SOE, MNC AND CPC

Negotiation styles vary from company to company. As a rough guide, expect a slow, traditional negotiation with an SOE, something speedier and more Western with an MNC, and from a

Table 9.1 *Different Perceptions and Negotiation Procedures*

	Chinese	Western
Negotiation focuses on:	Process	Content
	Means	End
	Generalities	Specifics
The outcome is:	Trust	Legal contract
A contract is:	A summary of discussion	Binding legal document
	A "snapshot of the relationship"	Open to Change
Fairness is assessed by:	Procedure	Outcomes

Adapted from Ming-Jer Chen, Inside Chinese Business (2001).

CPC – well, that depends on the character of the boss. Such a person will be more likely to be businesslike and not bureaucratic, but at the same time trust and emotion may matter to them a great deal. But there are no hard and fast rules here: treat every CPC boss as a different individual. Table 9.1 illustrates the differences between Western and Chinese negotiating philosophies.

NEGOTIATING EFFECTIVELY WITH THE CHINESE

Finally we would like to summarize some of the necessary actions to take to negotiate successfully in China. Wei Wang (2006) suggests these five stages to negotiate effectively:

Stage 1: Team preparation
Stage 2: Negotiation preparations
Stage 3: Maintaining emotional balance
Stage 4: Adopt both Chinese and Western perspectives
Stage 5: Adopt a combination of Western and Chinese behaviors

In Stage 1, the preparing of the team, needs to be thorough and consists of the following:

a) The negotiating team should be prepared in terms of understanding China's historical and social context to better understand where the Chinese are coming from; be a group with solid intellectual qualities; and finally, individual members need to be emotionally balanced and have inner strength. The last point is crucial because any frustrations displayed in an aggressive manner will be perceived by the Chinese as loss of face and will jeopardize the negotiations

b) The team needs to comprise highly competent and technical experts in their own field, have their own interpreters who ideally are not only competent linguistically, but also have worked in both the West and China. Perhaps more importantly, the leader needs to show both IQ and EQ (emotional intelligence) qualities in order to sustain the rigors of negotiations. The leader should have the authority to make decisions and thereby ensure his credibility

c) Finally, the team should be mentally prepared for long haul, which could last from a few months to years. Our own experience with a SOE took us about two years before we finally closed the deal

The second stage is Negotiation Preparations, comprising the following:

a) There needs to be a thorough intelligence appraisal of your counterpart, drawn from various published sources, consultants, trade publications, etc. This thoroughness will be appreciated by the Chinese and will enhance your standing and influence with them.

b) Your team will need to be very clear on its negotiating position: What is the bottom line? Are your targets clearly realistic and defined? What are you willing to compromise on? What can you "give" or concede to the Chinese? (Such "give-aways" help the negotiating process and engender goodwill.)

c) Finally, your team should have all the necessary support materials such as company brochures, name cards, audiovisual material, etc. If they are all translated into Chinese, this will be a huge boost to your chances of winning a bid. Furthermore, bringing small but inexpensive gifts which are symbolic of Western culture is considered very favorably by the Chinese, as it indicates that you respect the Chinese cultural tradition and are making the effort; and that you are willing to develop friendly relationships.

The third stage is maintaining emotional balance: this refers to members of your team not expressing emotional outbursts because of the slow pace of the proceedings or obstacles that your team consider minor, and so on. This is a serious point as any emotional display that smacks of aggression, annoyance etc. will jeopardize the negotiations and lose the respect of the Chinese. Outward display of emotions is seen as loss of face in China. There are a number of ways to prepare for this:

a) Anticipate frustrations, prolonged delays and walking out of the negotiations without a signed deal.

b) Allow time in your schedule. Educate your headquarters of the long-term nature of negotiations in China; accept that the Chinese are not that familiar with Western legal and regulatory rules, that the Chinese negotiators especially from SOEs, have bureaucratic constraints to deal with before decisions can be made and therefore progress takes time. You should build in time to understand where the Chinese are coming from, what is their mindset, etc; all this will help you and your team to maintain emotional balance.

c) Finally, thinking strategically in the heat of the moment is always very helpful. This enables you to distance yourself from the minutiae of the negotiating process.

The fourth stage is to try to adopt both Western and Chinese perspectives in the negotiating process, otherwise it is more than likely that the negotiations will grind to a halt. This can be achieved by:

a) Deconstructing some of your preconceived myths and assumptions about the Chinese such as that they are untruthful, deceptive (which was discussed extensively in Chapter 4), that they are susceptible to logical arguments (when in fact, some emotional intelligence will work wonders here), and so on.

b) Attempt to understand the Chinese perspective, in particular, the core Chinese cultural values governing behavior; such as a tendency to follow the leader, an indirect communications style, having a long-term view, and a need to save face, so please do not try and solicit candid feedback in a meeting with them. Of course, again we need to be cautious when making these recommendations, as it depends who is in the Chinese team, there could be different generations, others with Western experience, etc. You need to make a judgment call on how to approach the situation. As they say in China "It depends..." – on whom you are talking to, where in China..., what you are talking about..., etc. Finally, we believe that if you spend some time on understanding non-communication behavior, this will reap huge rewards when dealing with the Chinese.

The final fifth stage involves employing a combination of Chinese and Western behaviors in order to be effective. In other words, mirroring behavior is a powerful way to overcome some of the cultural obstacles. In general, the Western approach is direct communication, logical thinking, achievement-driven, confrontational if necessary, and so on, whereas the Chinese approach is different. They want the same outcomes but do so in a different manner, their behavior is driven by the need to build relationships in negotiations, having frank discussions with a face-saving approach. Any difficulties can be overcome by using some oriental wisdom: as our parents used to say, "Sometimes it's quicker to take the side road to reach your destination." Many of these points have been discussed in this book already and will not be elaborated here.

Remember that at the end of the day, Chinese negotiators, like their Western counterparts, do want the final goals and ends. Be patient.

10
Coaching and Psychometrics

As this book is mainly for those who work with Chinese people, we will look at coaching from the perspective of "Leader as a Coach" rather than from that of the professional coach.

Chinese people still don't know what to make of coaching. There is no single Chinese word for it. We once asked a leadership training class of Chinese managers in an MNC "How do you feel when your foreign manager wants to coach you?" and got the following replies:

- "I feel that he wants to teach me something."

- "I feel that he wants to tell me something."

- "What's wrong with me?"

- "I feel I am humiliated, it implies that I am useless."

If this is what Chinese managers working for MNCs responded, imagine what Chinese managers working for SOEs or CPCs would say...

Coaching was introduced to China in the late 1990s, and the first generation of Chinese coaches emerged in 2003. At this time some MNCs and CPCs started to send their managers on more formal coaching programs. It did not generate much interest at the time. The Chinese believe that personal development is through education, and the concept of education in China is the "spoon-feed" lecture given by academic scholars in a classroom.

One of the authors was asked by the Europe-based headquarters of a MNC in China to conduct a coaching session for one of their high flyers, a Chinese director in Beijing. I found it a bit strange that the local HR did not get in touch with me on this matter.

Again, the headquarters arranged for me to meet the CEO of China for further discussions. I arrived at the CEO's office on time, but the HR Manager had not come by the time we were supposed to start the meeting. To me as a Chinese, the CEO was a tall and strong European; he looked quite serious and tense. During the waiting time for the HR Manager to arrive, I initiated a chat about his impression of China to relax both of us. He said he loved China very much and his wife studied Chinese very hard, I realized that he had a warm heart towards China.

Fifteen minutes later than the appointed meeting time, his HR manager appeared. She said, "Oh, sorry, I am late. Do you think I need to be here?" The CEO said, "Yes, of course, we need to talk about coaching for one of our senior Chinese Managers."

His HR Manager looked very annoyed, "Frankly, I don't think we need coaching, the coach from headquarters did several sessions, but we did not benefit at all and just wasted time."

The CEO didn't introduce me to his HR Manager, and she did not appear that bothered about wanting to know who I was. I then introduced myself to her and asked her why she didn't find coaching useful.

She didn't answer me directly but excused herself, citing some urgent things to do. The CEO asked me to go ahead and sent me the coachee's contact details to start with.

My first session with the Chinese Director was basically just to relax him. He was in charge of the China sales team, he was very confident but very tense. I found out from him at the second session, that his Chinese colleagues also received coaching from either their foreign boss or an internal coach from headquarters. They were worried that coaching was just another way to check them out, they were very reluctant, actually quite frightened, to talk about their true feelings. That was why he was quite resistant and finally agreed to take coaching from an external and native speaking coach.

I conducted four sessions with the Chinese Director and he seemed much happier, more confident and relaxed by the end of it. We concluded our last session with the following conversation:

"What do you feel about this coaching process?"
"It is great, I feel very relaxed and comfortable talking through issues with you."
"Why?"
"Because I know the purpose of coaching me is only to help me."

Training became accepted as another way of personal development in China in the late 1990s. At that time the training market was booming to satisfy office workers' thirst for management knowledge, which was then not part of university education. This training tended to be of the "academic lecture" type. Since then, it has moved on, through being a kind of entertaining show to modern action learning.

In recent years, coaching has prevailed at MNCs among Western managers who benefit from it as a tool for personal development. Coaching has been pushed into China for local talent development. However, because Chinese staff do not understand it, they don't think that it is worth taking time for one-to-one coaching.

Western managers are often disappointed that their Chinese peers are not excited about coaching as they expected. Some get frustrated that their Chinese managers either keep postponing the start date of being coached or don't bother to coach their teams. Why? Well, imagine that you as a Westerner work for a Chinese company, and your Chinese manager asks you to practice "the golden mean" at work. If you don't understand the concept, you won't do anything with it: this is what your Chinese managers think about coaching.

It also does not help that some foreign coaches lack knowledge of or sensitivity to Chinese culture; they conduct coaching for Chinese staff in the same way as for Westerners with no respect for cultural differences. And then, of course, language creates a barrier: few coaches are native Chinese speakers. But the biggest problem is that certain aspects of the "ideology" of coaching just don't fit with Chinese culture.

- *One-to-one*. Equality is critical in the "one-to-one" coaching set up. But a sense of hierarchy is part of the Chinese "gene" and exists everywhere. So most Chinese cannot but see one-to-one coaching as "superior-to-subordinate" directing.

- *The Coach as an objective nonexpert*. A common practice in Chinese organizations is that the manager is an expert in the field; for example the president of a hospital has to be the best doctor first. The concept of "expert leader" is part of Chinese mindset, coming from Confucius's belief in "scholar superiority." CPCs are beginning to accept professional managers, following MNC practice, but SOEs still retain "expert-oriented" management. In general, a manager who is an amateur in the technical field in which his or her team is engaged will find extreme difficulty in winning respect. The same goes for a coach. "If this person does not understand the technicalities of what I do, how can they understand my issues?"

- *Asking questions*. Asking the "right question" at the right time is a core coaching skill. But being asked questions is not good news in China. If your leader asks you questions, it may imply that he/she is not happy with you or even distrusts you. The person being asked would be very cautious in how he/she replies. They will certainly not answer quickly and straight from the heart, as the ideal coaching client does.

- *Not providing solutions*. In coaching, the client is expected to find the answers to their own problems – coaching isn't mentoring, it is the creation of a "space" where people can discover their own solutions. But in China, providing solutions is the "divine right" as well as the obligation of the leader. The "obligation" part is important. The dispassionate coach, helping the client along the road of their own decision making, is seen as weak and unhelpful, maybe even tricky.

- *Listening.* This is the most difficult thing for Chinese managers; "Listen to your parents, listen to your teacher and listen to your leader" is the credo derived from Confucianism in the Chinese mindset. Yet it seems there is a "leadership curse" when a person seems to automatically lose half of his/her listening ability as soon as he/she becomes a team leader. And he or she can only listen to their superior, no longer to subordinates. Ironically, when the subordinate is allowed to talk freely, the subordinate may now worry about "What's wrong with my boss?" or "What's his or her hidden agenda."

- *Giving neutral feedback.* Coaching feedback should be neutral and nonjudgmental. However, this is a real challenge for Chinese managers as we don't have many neutral words in our language. Chinese terms are either positive or negative. Even with English words, we tend to categorize them in the same way. Furthermore, being "judgmental" (a deadly sin in coaching) is regarded in China as good: it shows one has analytical ability and insight. The traditional Chinese way of giving feedback is more critical than appreciative – as one SOE manager put it, "We perceive criticism as positive feedback. At least it means the leader is paying attention to us."

- *Self-awareness.* This is another golden tenet of coaching that leaves the Chinese cold. The Chinese believe more in self-cultivation than self-awareness, which is not seen as having much point.

- *Trust.* Coaching is based on this, but in China this is always a sensitive nerve, until you have really good *guānxì* with someone. A leader needs to take time to "slowly cook" his or her own credibility in the team and gain trust before rushing into the coaching feast.

By now, hopefully, you will appreciate your Chinese colleagues' complex feelings towards coaching.

Of course, putting you off coaching is not our intention. To the contrary, if you understand these assumptions in your Chinese colleagues' minds and are willing to practice coaching in a Chinese way, it will be hugely rewarding for both you and the company.

We have much experience of coaching Chinese mangers. It takes a longer time to warm up but they can be just as open and appreciative as Westerners, as long as they realize the purpose of self-development and get in tune with the coach.

INTRODUCING COACHING

Before you talk or do anything related to coaching, it is a good idea to set up a team meeting to give an introduction to coaching, to make clear the purpose, principles, attitudes, skills and methodology of coaching, and to explain the difference between coaching and training.

Looking at these in greater depth...

Purpose

- Raise self-awareness: it is a journey to understand yourself. What are you doing now? What do you want to do? What do you want to be? What are your strengths and in what areas do you need to improve?

- To help you to find your untapped potential.

- To help you to take more responsibility for finding your own solutions to your challenges.

Principles

- Equality. It is not the relationship of superior–subordinate, older–younger or experienced–inexperienced; it is an equal conversation between peers.

- "Coach" is a role not a position: people within a team can coach each other.

- Confidentiality: keep the conversation to yourself only, unless by agreement with your counterpart.

Attitude

- Open minded

- Empathetic

- Neutral and nonjudgmental

Skills

- Asking question: 30 percent of coaching time.

- Listening: 60 percent of coaching time.

- Giving feedback: 10 percent of coaching time.

Methodology

There are various ways to conduct coaching. The GROW model (John Whitmore) as illustrated in Figure 10.1 is one of the popular methods. You can use this model to demonstrate coaching skills to your team.

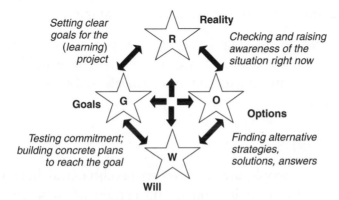

Figure 10.1 *The "GROW" model of coaching*

To develop a habit of coaching, we would suggest that you use coffee time as a coaching opportunity in a social way.

PSYCHOMETRICS

Psychometric instruments were developed in the West on the basis of Western psychology, but in fact, we have found that they actually work better for Chinese than Westerners.

Psychology is fashionable in China at the moment: there are numerous psychological programs on TV mainly for helping people with relationship, marriage or family issues. To some viewers, psychology is seen as kind of "Western version of magic spells" rather than science – but "magic spells" have always been popular in China!

In our experience, most Chinese managers are excited about the result of their psychometric assessments. For most of them, it is the first time they have seen their "self" through the lens of Western science. They are convinced by the results.

Thus, psychometrics is a very effective way to conduct coaching for your Chinese colleagues; however, be cautious on the following points:

- Select simple and easily understood psychometric instruments, as most Chinese lack basic knowledge of psychology. Myers Briggs Type Indicator (MBTI); Fundamental Interpersonal relation Orientation behavior (Firo-B); Strength Deployment Inventory (SDI) and DISC are good examples.

- The person feeding back the assessment result must be professionally qualified because the language used in feedback has an impact on a coachee's self-image and self-concept.

BUZZ WORDS

In the West, people are all used to psychological buzz-words. This is not the case in China, and certain of these can cause misunderstandings.

- *Challenge*: This word in Chinese can be negative and aggressive. It implies provocation, strong disagreement, even physical threat, as in "I challenge you to a fight."

   In a board meeting between foreign and Chinese parties, a foreign director said to a Chinese director, "I would like to challenge you on that..." The Chinese director stormed out of the room.

   It is useful to explain that "challenge" is a positive word, designed to stimulate thinking or to turn a problem into an opportunity.

- *Reflect*: This is another word can be perceived in a very negative way in China. It carries the implication that a mistake has been made and the reflector needs to sit down, close the door and think what he or she has done wrong and why people think it is so bad. "Further thinking" or "deep thinking" are better terms to use.

- *Empathy*: The common pitfall is that empathy is seen as being synonymous with sympathy. Even some English-Chinese dictionaries translate these two words as same meaning. "Put yourself into others' shoes" or "feel what others feel" is a better way of expressing the concept.

- *Feedback*: Chinese are used to giving opinions and advice, which are subjective. Objective feedback is often confused with this. Clarify this in advance.

CONCLUSION

Conducting effective coaching for Chinese people is tough; it requires patience, understanding of cultural background, and sensitivity of language.

As a team leader, informal coaching will be much more effective than formal. It is not easy for Chinese to openly talk about personal feelings; we are relatively more tense and serious at our workplace. The mindset of hierarchy and authority is always with us.

So start by infusing the coaching mindset, nurturing the coaching culture, and then structure your coaching around a specific task and create a relaxing environment. This will help your team members unlock their potential.

Conclusion

China is perhaps now the leading country for companies entering its market in huge numbers and where opportunities abound in that market. China is indeed an exciting market, yet equally it is a complex one because it is a society undergoing a massive transition in the context of the oldest surviving culture, and a large state sector and consequently a large bureaucracy. Trying to negotiate your way around this myriad bureaucracy is a daunting challenge. Also, it is one of the largest and fastest-growing emerging economies in the world, and such rapid development brings along its unique set of challenges and problems, such as unbalanced growth, pollution, lack of transparency, limited business regulations as the state tries to catch up with developments, and so on. Under these circumstances, it becomes difficult for corporations and businessmen operating in this market. Difficult as it may be, it is not insurmountable: as the Chinese saying has it: "everything is difficult, but everything is possible."

However, China's phenomenal economic growth is equally matched by its increasing flexibility and practicality in the business arena in terms of attempting to adapt their business methodologies to "best practices" in the world. This is encouraging and will undoubtedly help those Chinese companies to blend their Chinese practices with the best Western tools and methods. Equally important, is that foreign companies operating in China will also need to adapt their Western best practices to suit the Chinese cultural environment.

In this book, we have attempted to illustrate the importance of Chinese leadership and culture for foreign managers and businesses if they want to be effective in the Chinese market. Therefore, to be successful, one needs to understand and learn a little about Chinese ways and mindset. We believe that having some basic knowledge of Chinese history and culture is invaluable; and that once you are in China, you should continue your learning. Only in this way will you come a little closer to understanding the Chinese and people you will be working with. Having said this, we are not advocating that every foreign manager needs to learn a huge amount about the Chinese way. Not only is this not feasible but it's also impractical; all we are saying is that they be aware that there are attitudes and practices that have to adapt to the Chinese way, though, equally, there are Western attitudes and practices that need to be adopted in China. Implicit in our position is that not all management and leadership tools and methodologies are universally applicable; nor are highly developed analytical tools and techniques always essential to ensure business success. Business success in this market is appreciating the need to balance the best of Western management and analytical practices with ancient Chinese leadership and cultural wisdom. As China's economy becomes more integrated with the world economy, this need becomes more imperative.

Last but not least, we have tried to present our ideas with a clarity that is easily understood and digestible. There is a Chinese saying which goes like this: "The expert can summarize one subject in two pages, the master can do it in two sentences, and the sage can do it in one word." The best scholar in China is normally one who can turn profound knowledge into a simple message for the audience.

We are not sure how much we could achieve in this rather short book, given that Chinese culture and leadership has always been seen as complicated and mysterious, although now, hopefully, the reader will have caught a glimpse of this unveiled ancient nation. This brings to mind the old story about six blind men who were introduced to an elephant and asked to figure out what it was they were touching. Metaphorically speaking, if you were one of the "blind" people who touched the part of an elephant to figure out its whole image, we hope you have finally seen it.

Strong features and important qualities of the Chinese language are its ambiguity and its philosophical overtones. People can perceive and interpret the same word or concept quite differently; furthermore, the evolution of the Chinese language has made the ancient language which all the classic texts were written in even more obscure. There is an ongoing debate now amongst Chinese scholars on specific meanings of some key values such as "*dào*," "*rén*," and "*zhōng yōng*." Consequently, Chinese leaders exercise their leadership with their own understanding of Chinese values that probably make the Westerner feel lost in a multi-faceted Chinese race.

However, leadership is an art, you cannot be too rational to understand it; improving your emotional intelligence (EQ) will help you a great deal. This is especially so as the Chinese believe that we are an artistic and romantic nation; in China we always prefer "Leader as *jūnzǐ*," whereas in the West it is "Leader as Coach." Also, the Chinese often refer to the "art of leading" rather than "leadership," and "balance", the maintenance of harmonious dynamics is the fine art of "Chinese leadership."

About the Authors

BARBARA XIAOYU WANG (BA, MBA)

Barbara is a Programme Director at Ashridge Business School, as well as being its China Representative. Her interests are in leadership and executive coaching and she has extensive experience in management training and consulting.

She has conducted corporate training for major organizations such as Novartis, VW, Ericsson, BP, MARS, TCL, Akzo Nobel, ICBC, etc. Barbara has also run training and coaching programs bilingually in English and Mandarin for companies such as ABB, Danfoss, Volvo, Daimler, Sinopec, China Post, OCS, Air Canada, Industrial & Commercial Bank of China etc; as well as teaching on MBA programmes in Chinese universities.

Before Ashridge, Barbara was a Vice President for the Western Management Institute of Beijing; and her commercial experience extends to working for multinational companies in China where she was the Retail Operations Manager for CELINE of the Louis Vuitton group; the Global Accounts Manager in China at DHL, and Assistant to the General Manager at the Swissôtel, Beijing.

Barbara has graduated with a BA and MBA; and is qualified in leadership psychometric tools such as FIRO-B, Strength Deployment Inventory (SDI), profiler 360, MBTI (Myers Briggs Type Indicator) as well as being a certified coach from the LMI (Leadership Management International. USA).

HAROLD CHEE (MBA, MSc, MA, BA, DMS, DipEcon)

Harold is a Programme Director at Ashridge Business School (UK) and his expertise is leadership, cross-cultural management and marketing strategy. He is also an executive coach and is qualified in psychometric instruments such as FIRO-B, SDI (Strength Deployment Inventory), MBTI, and 360 Profiler. At Ashridge, he teaches a portfolio of courses such as the MBA, Strategy and Leadership, and Developing Business and Leadership Skills.

Harold has worked internationally with a diverse range of clients including Philips, Volvo, China Post, Rexam, Continental, ITT Industries, Volkswagen, Lufthansa, Degussa, BBC, Roche Pharmaceuticals, PricewaterhouseCoopers, Glaxosmithkline, Tetra Pak, Reserve Banks of Zimbabwe and Swaziland, and the Bank of Scotland. He works extensively in China with clients such as ABB, Novartis, Swire Beverages, Siemens, Daimler, China International Capital Corporation, and Sinopec.

Prior to Ashridge, he worked as a Business Development Manager and Chief Trainer for the China–Britain Management Training Centre; as an Organizational Development manager for the Anglo-American Corporation in Zimbabwe and South Africa conducting assignments in change management and strategic change; as a university lecturer for several years in the UK; and in marketing for several organisations.

He is an economics graduate and among his publications are: "Investing in China or the UK?" in *Globalisation Laid Bare* (Industry & Parliament Trust Publications, 2009); *The Myths of Doing Business in China* (2nd edition, Macmillan 2007) and *Global Marketing Strategies* (Financial Times/Pitman, 1998).

References and Further Reading

Introduction

Franke, H. Richard, Hofstede, Geert and Bond, Michael H. (1991) "Cultural Roots of Economic Performance: A Research Note," *Strategic Management Journal*, 2: 165–73.

Redding, S. Gordon (1982) "Cultural effects on the Marketing process in Southeast Asia," *Journal of the Market Research Society*, 24: 2: 98–114.

Chapter 1

King-Hall, Stephen (1924) *Western Civilization and the Far East*. London, Methuen.

Chapter 2

Chen, Chao-Chuan, and Lee, Yueh-Ting (eds) (2008) *Leadership and Management in China: Philosophies, Theories, and Practices*. Cambridge University Press.

Chapter 3

Crow, C. (1937) *400 Million Customers*. New York, Halcyon.

Chapter 4

Yue-er, Luo, Duerring. E and Byham W. C. (2008) *Leadership Success in China: An Expatriate's Guide*. Pittsburgh, DDI Press.

Chapter 6

Hall, E. T. (1976) *Beyond Culture*. Garden City, NY: Anchor Press.

Chapter 9

Chen, Ming-Jer (2001) *Inside Chinese Business*. Boston, HBS Press.
Wang, Wei (2006) *The China Executive*. Peterborough, 2W Publishing.

Further Reading

Allinson. R. E. (1991) *Understanding the Chinese Mind*. Oxford University Press.
Ambler, T., Witzel, M., and Chao. X (2009) *Doing Business in China* (3rd ed). London, Routledge.
Bond, M. H. (1991) *Beyond the Chinese Face: Insights from Psychology*. Oxford University Press.
Bond, M. H. (ed) (1986) *The Psychology of the Chinese People*. Oxford University Press.
Brahm, L. J. (2003) *When YES means NO!* Boston, Tuttle.
Bucknall, K. (1994) *Cultural Guide to Doing Business in China*. Oxford, Butterworth-Heinemann.
Chang, G. (2002) *The Coming Collapse of China*. London, Century Publications.
Chao-Chuan, Chen and Lee, Yueh-Ting (2008) *Leadership and Management in China*. Cambridge University Press.
Chee, H. and West. C. (2007) *Myths About Doing Business in China* (2nd ed). Basingstoke, Palgrave Macmillan.
Chen, Dongsheng (2006) *The Original Wisdom of Chinese Management*. Beijing, Enterprise Management Publishing House.
Chen, Ming-Jer (2001) *Inside Chinese Business*. Boston, HBS Press.
Chu, Chin-Ning (1991) *The Asian Mind Game*. New York, Rawson.
Cleary, T. (1988) *Sun Tsu's Art of War*. Boston, Shambhala.

Cleary, T. (1999) *Ways of the Warriors, Codes of Kings: Lessons in leadership from the Chinese Classics.* Boston, Shambhala.

Confucius (2006) *The Analects.* Beijing. China Press.

Crow, C. (1937) *400 Million Customers.* New York, Halcyon.

De Mente. B. L. (1992) *Chinese Etiquette and Ethics in Business.* Lincolnwood, NTC Business Books.

Fang, T. (1999) *Chinese Business Negotiating Style.* Thousand Oaks CA, Sage.

Feng Youlan (2009) *Chinese Contemporary Philosophy: Life, Reading, Knowledge.* Trinity Press.

Gallo, F. T. (2008) *Business Leadership in China.* Singapore, John Wiley & Sons (Asia).

Gittings, J. (2005) *The Changing Face of China: From Mao to Market.* Oxford University Press.

Goodfellow, R., Wang, K., and Sheng, Z. X. (1998) *Chinese Business Culture.* Oxford, Butterworth-Heinemann.

Griffith, S. B. (1963) *Sun Tzu: The Art of War.* New York, Oxford University Press.

Hall, E. T. (1976) *Beyond Culture.* Garden City, NY: Anchor Press.

Hofstede, G. (1994) *Cultures and Organizations.* London, HarperCollins Business.

Hou, W. C., and Luh, L. L. (1998) *The 36 Strategies of the Chinese.* Singapore, Addison Wesley Longman.

Kenna, P., and Lacy, S. (1994) *Business China: A Practical Guide to Understanding Chinese Business Culture.* New York, Contemporary Publishing House.

Kirkbride, P. S., Tang, S. F., and Westwood, R. I. (1991) "Chinese Conflict Preferences and Negotiating Behaviour: Cultural and Psychological Influences," *Organisation Studies,* 12(3): 365–86.

Kynge, J. (2006) *China Shakes the World.* London, Weidenfeld & Nicolson.

Lao Zi (2009) *Dào De Jing.* Beijing, Huaxia Press.

Levine, H. (2006) *Executive Leadership in China.* London, Heidrick & Struggles International.

Lin Yutang (2002) *The Wisdom of Chinese Sages*. Shanxi Normal University Press.

Mears, I. (1971) *Lao Zi: Dào De Jing (Tao The King)*. London, Theosophical Publishing House.

Munro. D. J. (1979) *The Concept of Man in Contemporary China*. Ann Arbor, University of Michigan Press.

Nan Huaijin (2002) *By-talk of Yijing*. Fudan University Press.

Qin Shan (2011) "Chinese Entrepreneurs: Influence of MNC Managers," *Chinese Entrepreneurs Journal*, Volume 1.

Redding, S. G. (1993) *The Spirit of Chinese Capitalism*. Berlin, de Gruyter.

Scott. D. (2007) *China Stands Up*. London, Routledge.

Seligman, S. (2000) *Dealing with the Chinese*. London, Management Books.

Sheh Seow, W. (2003) *Chinese Leadership*. Singapore, Times Editions.

Sia, A. (1997) *The Chinese Art of Leadership*. Singapore, Asiapac.

Tang, J., and Ward. A. (2002) *The Changing Face of Management*. London, Routledge.

Tian Zhaoyuan and Tian Liang (2007) *The History of Commerce*. Shanghai, Shanghai Literature Press.

Wang, Wei (2006) *The China Executive*. Peterborough, 2W Publishing Ltd.

Wang, Xiaoxue (2010) "The Brief of Feature of Governing and the Current Value of Militarism," *Theory and Modernisation Journal* Volume 1.

Wei Jiafu (2006) *The Method and Art of leading of SOE Leaders*. Wenku.baidu.com.

Wilhelm. R. (1971) *The I Ching or Book of Changes*. London, Routledge & Kegan Paul Ltd.

Wong, Y. H and Leung, T. K. P (2001) *Guanxi: Relationship Marketing in a Chinese Context*. New York, International Business Press.

Xu Zhuoyun (2006) *Leadership from Historical Perspective*. Guangxi Normal University Press.

Yue-er Luo, Duerring. E., and Byham, W. C. (2008) *Leadership Success in China: An Expatriate's Guide*. Pittsburgh, DDI Press.

Zeng Shiqiang (2005) *Chinese Leadership*. Beijing University Press.

Zeng Shiqiang (2006) *Confucianism, Mohism, Legalism, Dàoism in Business*. Beijing, China Machine Press.

Zhang Shaoyu (2006) *The Outline of Militarism*. www.civillaw.com.cn.

Index